A Hoop of Threads & Longing

20 Ink-Drinking, Slow-Burning Romantasy Embroidery Projects

Hilary Leslie

QUARRY

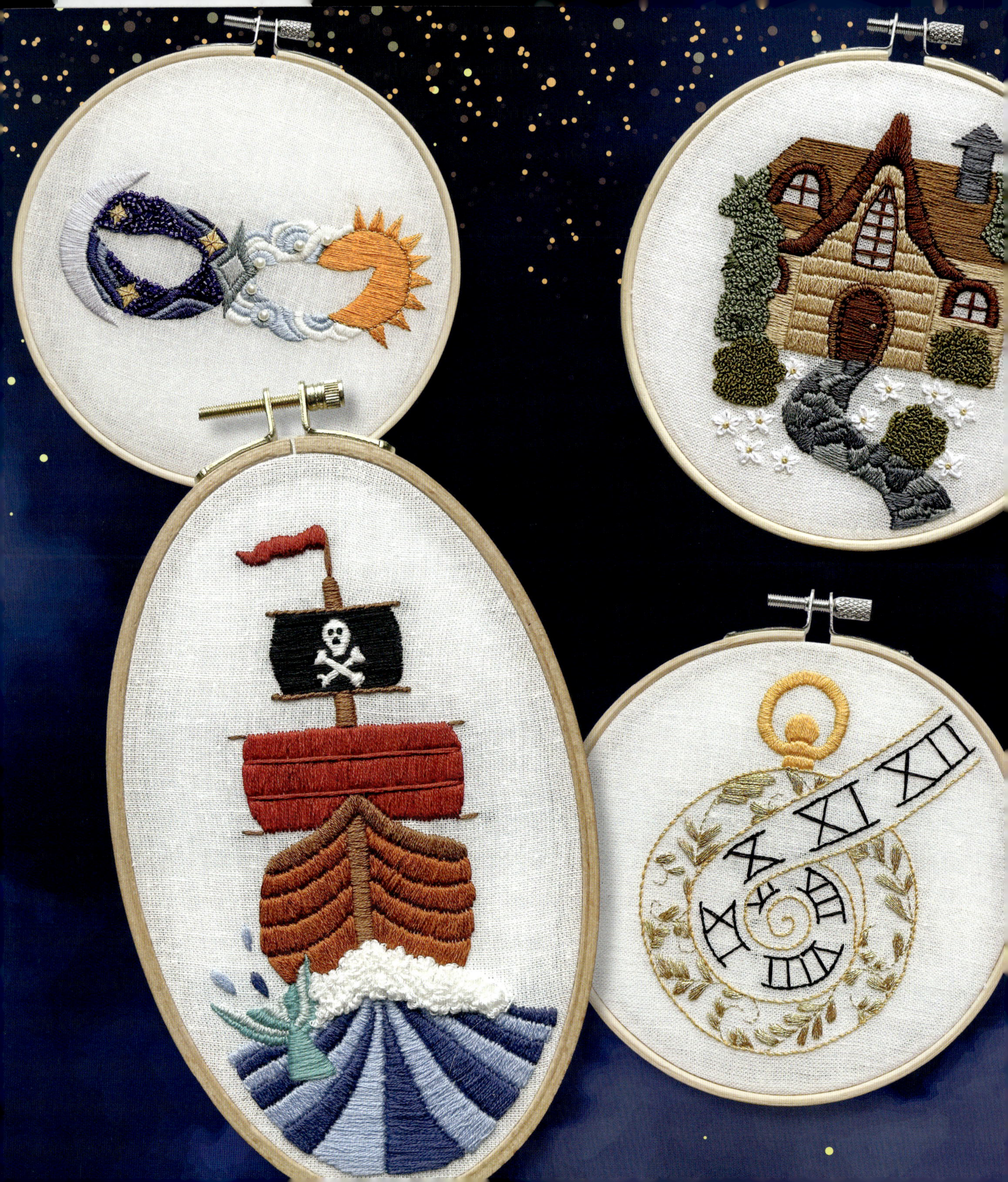

Contents

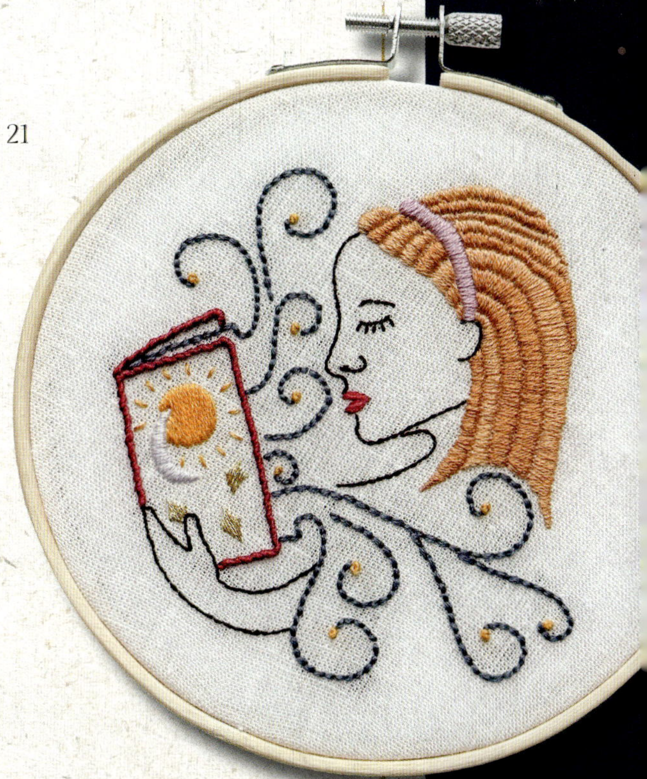

Your Journey Starts with a Single Stitch

Like many adults who rediscovered their love for reading and fantasy through the *A Court of Thorns and Roses* series, I (ten years late) was spellbound by the imaginary world of Prythian. My friend poked, prodded, and borderline begged me to start reading ACOTAR, eventually resorting to leaving the book at my house so I'd eventually dive in. Thanks to her, I started a new course in my creative life.

I've been embroidering for years, but I never expected a fantasy series to inspire my stitching. The first piece I created was the wolf from the cover. I love all the cover art from the series, drawn by Happy Pets, and when I posted my progress shots and videos, the response blew me away. The video showing the overall making of the hoop has almost two million views, and I learned very quickly just how beloved these stories are.

This book is my love letter to the romantasy genre. Whether you're here for morally gray love interests, the self-rescuing princess, or the dragon-riding rebel queens, I hope you'll find something in these pages that sparks your imagination—and your needle!

A Hoop of Threads & Longing isn't just about recreating my stitches. It's an invitation to experiment, to try new colors, add metallic threads, stitch with beads, or change up the background fabric. Many of the patterns are designed with flexibility in mind. They are perfect for bags, clothing, bookmarks, or anything you want to enchant with a bit of bookish magic.

Welcome to your next stitchery adventure! Let's thread our needles and dive in.

With love and longing,

Hilary

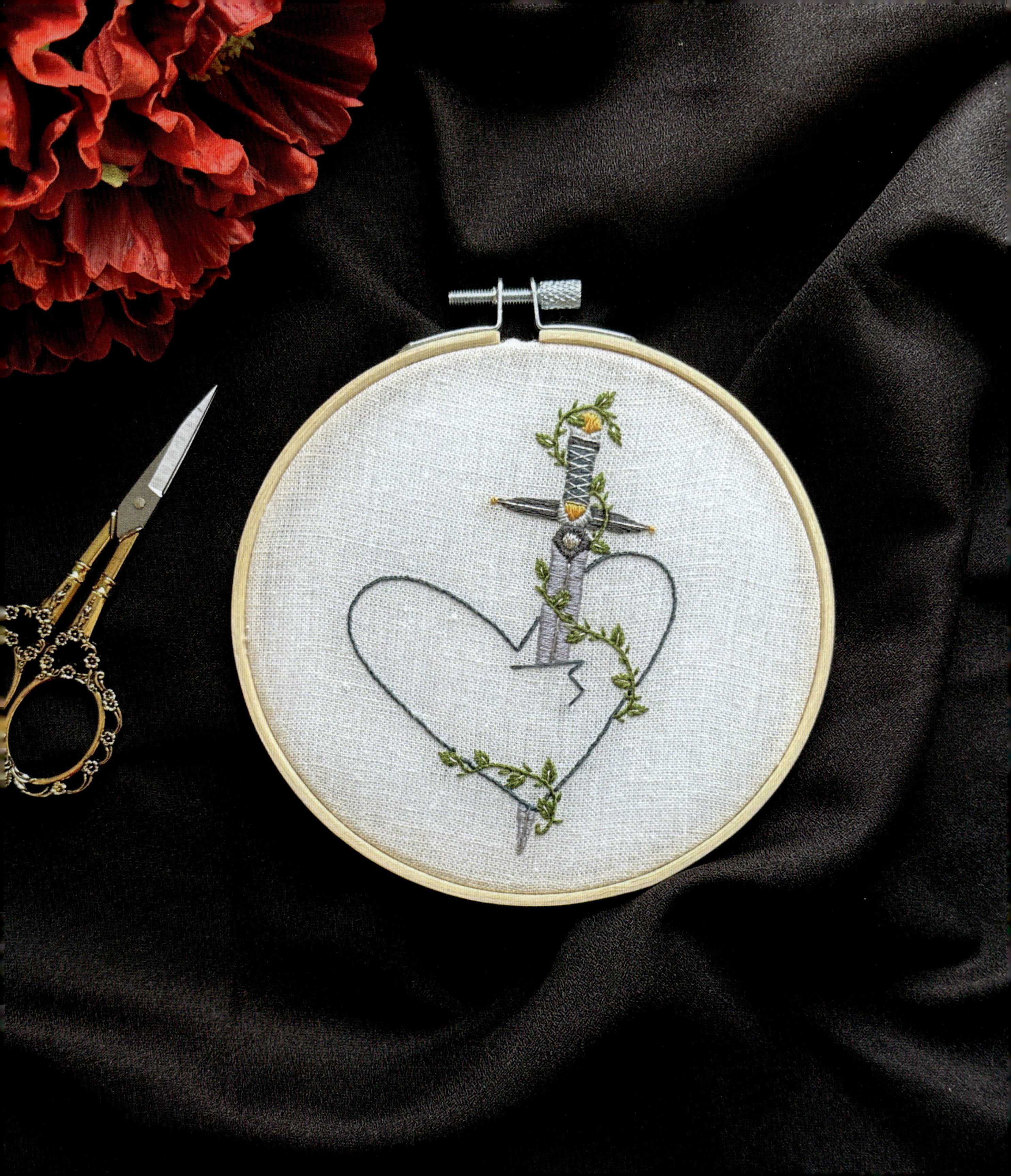

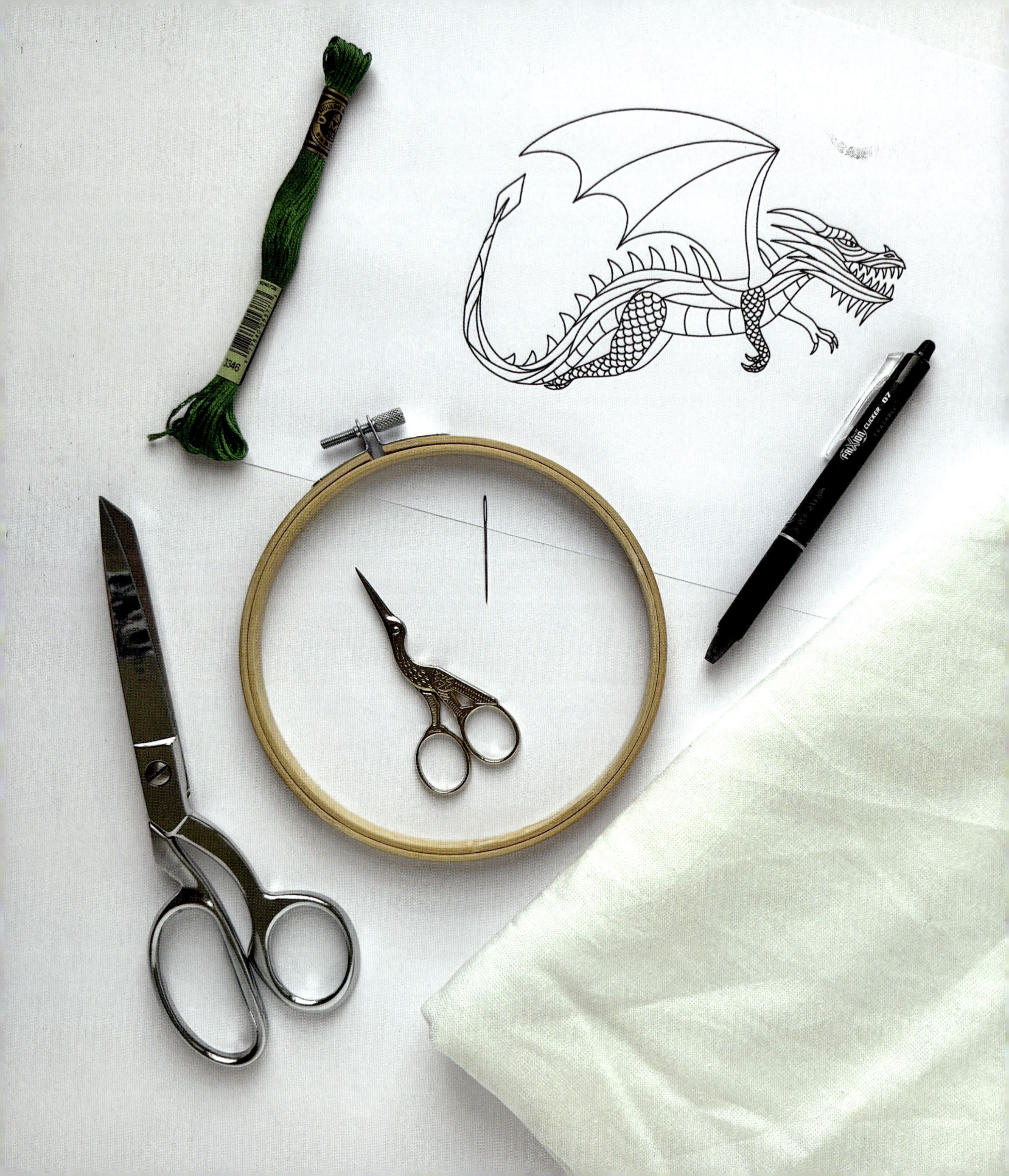
3346
FRIXION CLICKER 07

Getting Started

First things first, you'll need the right tools to get started on your embroidery journey. You can find supplies like these at your local craft stores, or you can order them online.

EMBROIDERY FLOSS

Embroidery floss is what will bring your design to life, and it comes in a myriad of beautiful colors! DMC is my preferred brand and is very popular among embroidery artists. DMC floss is made up of six individual strands. Using more strands creates a fuller, chunkier look, while fewer strands are great for fine detail work or thread painting. Match the color code on the floss label to the number provided in the pattern to recreate the exact look shown in this book. The Diamant colors (those that begin with D in the thread guides) are made of three very tightly spun plies. Treat this as a single stand. You should not try to separate these plies.

HOOPS

Embroidery hoops are what hold your fabric in place while you're stitching. They're available in a variety of sizes, measured based on their diameter from edge to edge. I prefer to work with bamboo hoops most of the time. I also love the faux wood options made by Anchor.

NEEDLES

There are many needle varieties you can use for embroidery depending on your project and comfort level! The eye of the needle—the opening through which you thread your floss—comes in many sizes. Embroidery needles have a smaller eye, while tapestry and chenille needles have a larger eye, which are great for projects using all six strands of floss or tapestry wool. Needle sizes vary as well—some are longer and thinner while others are shorter and thicker. Don't be afraid to experiment with different kinds!

SCISSORS

You'll need scissors not only to cut your embroidery floss throughout the stitching process but also to prep your fabric. Fabric scissors are very handy for cutting your fabric of choice with crisp lines. Embroidery scissors come in many sizes, with a variety of fun handles to express your personal style.

FABRIC

Fabric choice often comes down to personal preference, but you should be sure to buy cloth that doesn't stretch. Linen, my favorite to work with, is a popular choice, as is cotton. Don't be afraid to experiment with different colored fabrics, too! A colored fabric can make your stitching pop in contrast to colors you've chosen for embroidery floss.

Basic Techniques

After you've gathered your materials, it's time to prepare your hoop for stitching!

PREPARING YOUR HOOP

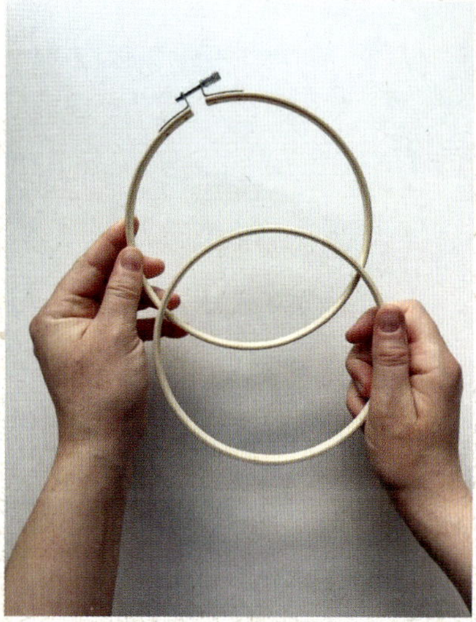

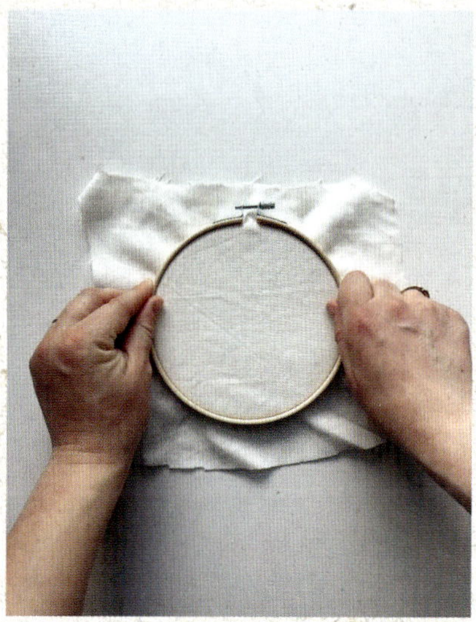

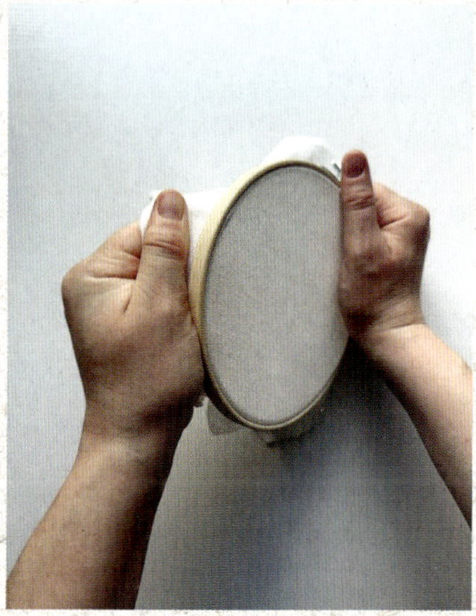

1. Unscrew the metal piece at the top of your outer hoop so you can separate the outer and inner hoops from each other.

2. Place a square of your fabric over the inner hoop (the smaller hoop and the hoop without the metal fastening). Then place the outer hoop over both the fabric and the inner hoop. Tightly screw the fastening at the top of your hoop.

3. Pull the edges of your fabric all the way around your hoop, so the fabric is very taut, like a drum. This not only aids in the pattern transfer process but also helps avoid puckering your fabric during stitching. Trim the edges of your cloth in a circle around your hoop with your fabric scissors. This will make it easier to stitch with clean, crisp edges.

TRANSFERRING YOUR DESIGN

Using a Paper Pattern

Using basic printer paper, you can print out your design to your preferred size. It should be no larger than the size of your hoop. Then, simply place your prepared hoop face down on the paper. Once you're happy with the placement, use your drawing tool of choice to trace the pattern onto the fabric. This technique works best with lighter-colored, transparent fabrics.

Using a Light Pad

If you have access to a light pad, laptop, tablet, or window, you can use it as a backlight to transfer your design. Place your printed pattern on top of the light source, then place your prepared hoop face down on top of the paper and start tracing right on the fabric. Again, you'll want to use light-colored fabrics for this technique.

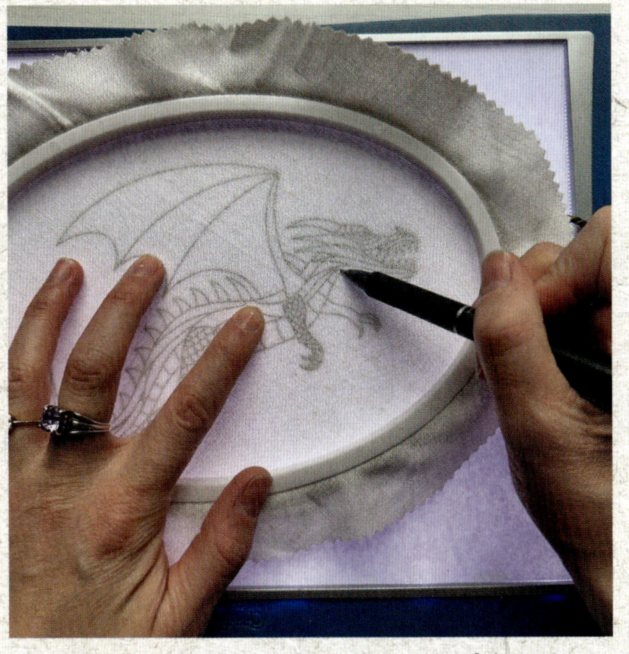

With your pattern transferred to your fabric, you're ready to start stitching!

Using a Digital Pattern

If you don't have a way to print out your pattern, you can trace it digitally! Open your PDF pattern and place your prepared hoop on the screen for tracing, whether you're using a laptop screen, tablet, or phone.

Other Transfer Methods

If you don't like to trace, there are alternative methods to get your pattern of choice onto your fabric. Stick-and-stitch paper (or water-soluble paper) comes in rolls and printer-friendly sheets. After printing your pattern onto the sheet, peel off the backing before placing the design directly onto your fabric. The pattern is stitched through the paper and the fabric. After you're finished, place the entire project under running water or in a bowl of water until all the paper dissolves away. Once your project has dried completely, you're finished!

Common Stitches

The patterns in this book use basic, beginner-friendly embroidery stitches. To help make the instructions even simpler, take note of when to push or pull the needle "up" and "down." "Up" means poking the needle through the back of the fabric and pulling up through to the front of the fabric. "Down" means pushing the needle through the front of the fabric/hoop and pulling it down through to the back of the fabric.

GETTING STARTED

Splitting Strands

DMC cotton floss, as well as many other brands, is made up of six individual strands. If a pattern calls for fewer than six strands, you'll need to split them apart. Dividing floss can be done a couple of ways: strand by strand or by groups of strands. Pay close attention to how many strands of floss each step in a pattern calls for to achieve the best finished result.

Threading Your Needle

When threading a needle with one to six strands of floss, cut about a forearm's length of embroidery floss and trim the very end with a pair of sharp scissors. A crisp end will make it easier to thread. Then, pass or "thread" the floss through the eye of the needle and pull through. Knot the end of the thread and start your stitching!

STITCH KEY

To keep things easy to follow, each project uses a stitch diagram with alphabetic references to identify the stitches used. Find more on reading the diagrams on page 18.

A Whipped backstitch
B Backstitch
C Satin stitch
D French knot
E Straight stitch
F Long and short stitch
G Fishbone stitch
H Lazy daisy stitch
I Chain stitch
J Loops

Scan the QR code to watch video tutorials of these common stitches.

Fastening Off Your Floss

When you're almost to the end of your thread, you need to fasten it to your project before cutting a new strand and continuing. Start by passing the needle down to the back of the work. Weave your needle through the stitches on the back of the work. Crisscross and pass the needle in different directions and through different stitches to secure it in place. Trim the excess floss.

WHIPPED BACKSTITCH (A)

The whipped backstitch is an extension of the backstitch and creates the look of a smooth line.

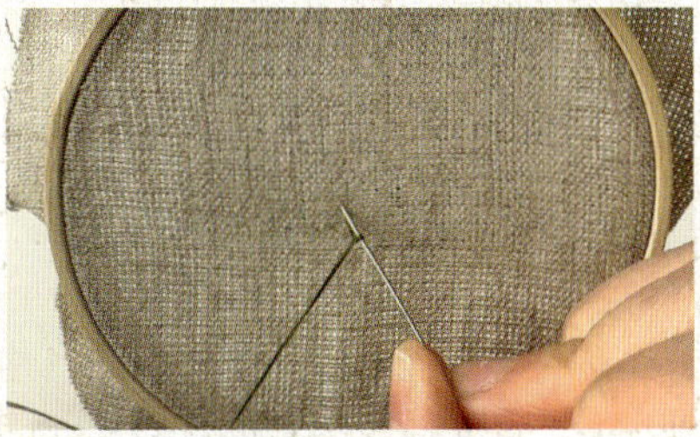

1. Follow instructions for the backstitch. With the needle pulled up through the end of the last stitch, weave the needle under the next backstitch from right to left, and pull the floss all the way through.

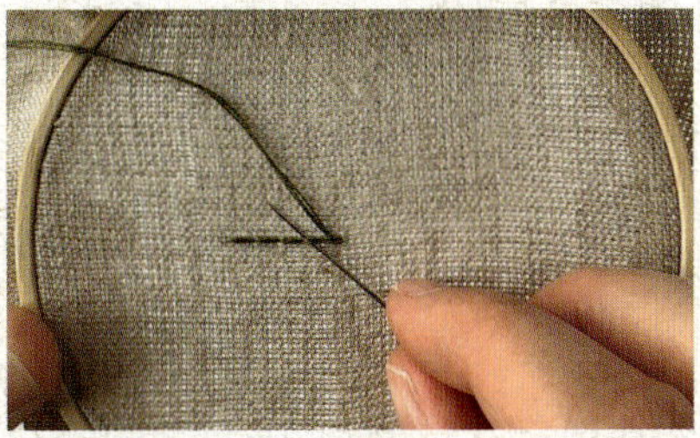

2. Weave the needle under the next backstitch, from right to left, and pull through. Continue like this for the entire length. Be sure to continue weaving under the backstitches in the same direction, from right to left.

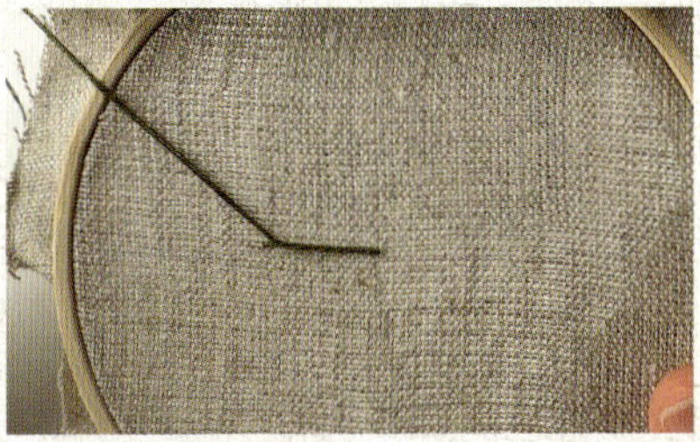

3. End the stitch by taking the needle down at the end of the line. Secure on back when finished.

BACKSTITCH (B)

The backstitch is a highly versatile stitch and a perfect one to learn as a complete beginner. This stitch can be used for outlining and lettering.

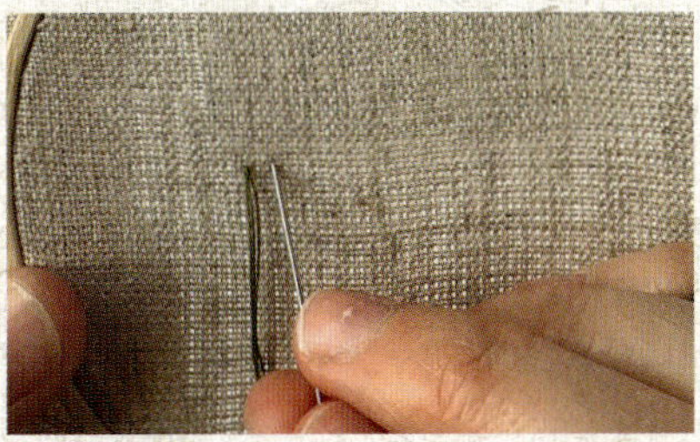

1. At the start of the line, go up until the knot stops the floss from going any farther. Go down through the fabric about ¼" (.5 cm) away from the first stitch.

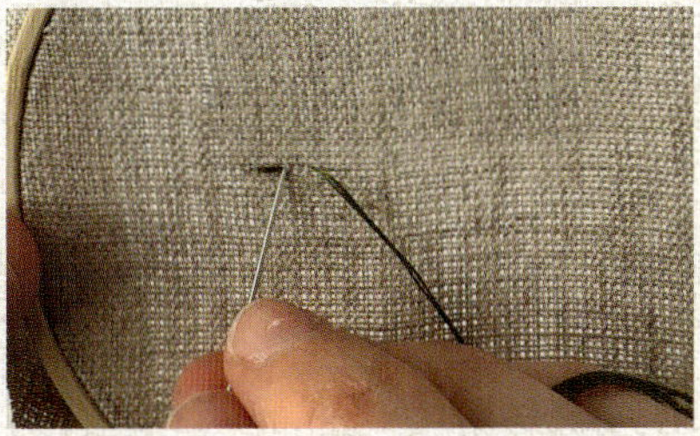

2. Go up through the fabric about ¼" (.5 cm) away from the previous stitch. Go down, meeting the floss from the previous stitch.

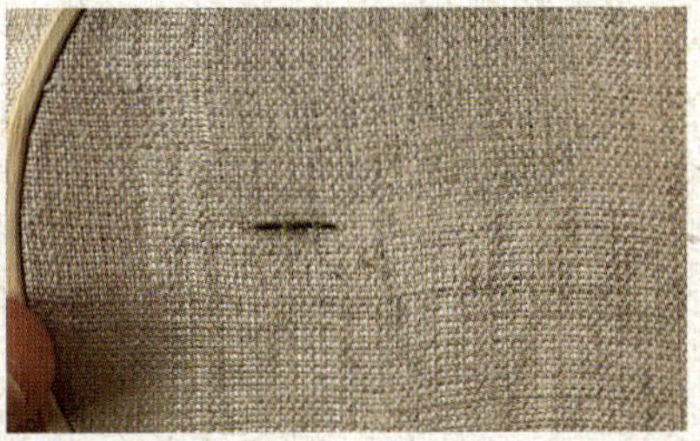

3. Continue all the way along the line or design section. Secure on back when finished.

SATIN STITCH (C)

Satin stitch is great for filling in larger areas of a design.

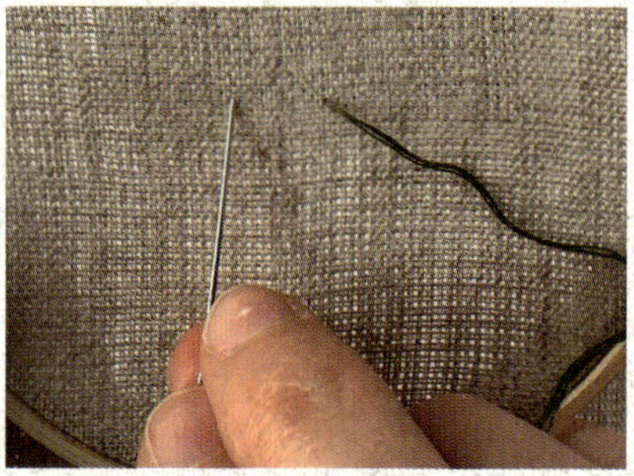

1. With needle threaded and a knot tied at the end, go up until the knot stops the floss from going any farther on one side of the area to be filled. Then, go down on the opposite edge of the area and pull all the way through.

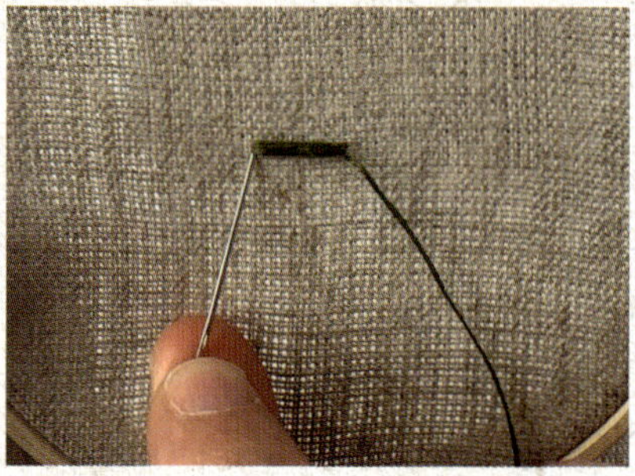

2. Go up again right next to the first stitch and continue this sequence, going edge to edge, filling up the empty space. Secure on back when finished.

Tip

Keep the stitches as close together as possible and make sure the floss doesn't twist between each stitch. Don't be afraid to take stitches out and start again if they start to overlap each other or have too much space between them.

FRENCH KNOT (D)

French knots create the look of tiny dots and are perfect for adding a starry texture to embroidery.

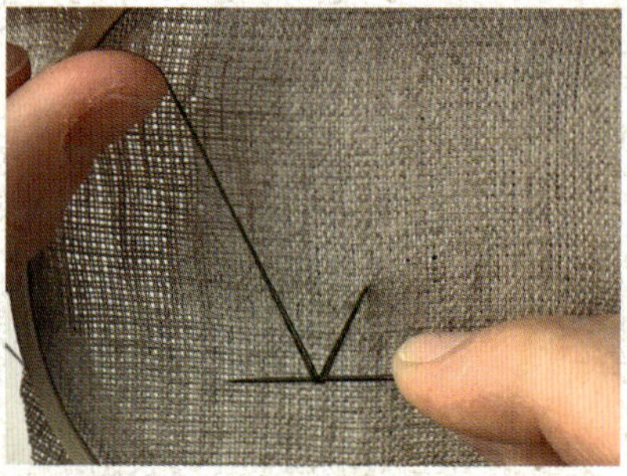

1. Go up until the knot stops the floss from going any farther. Hold the floss with one hand and the needle in the other, then wrap the needle one to three times.

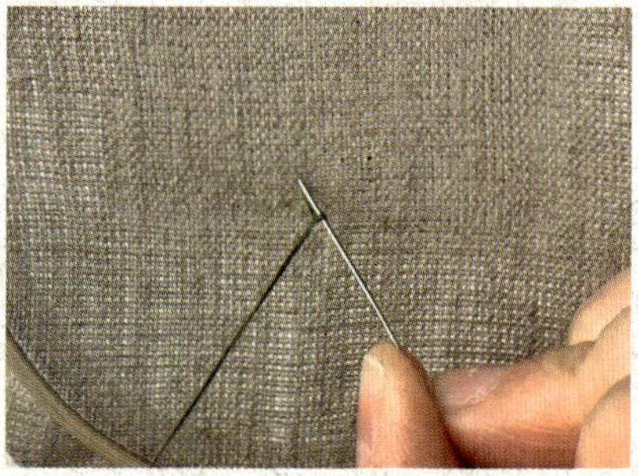

2. Hold the floss taut with one hand while the other directs the needle back down, close to the previous hole where the needle first came through.

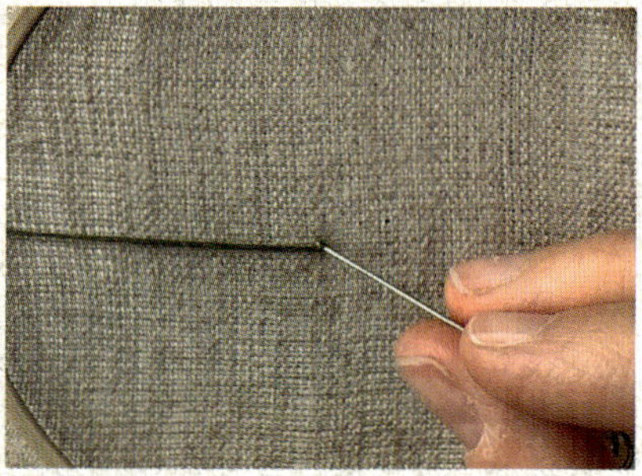

3. Pull all the way through to complete the knot. Secure on back when finished.

Tip Holding tension on the floss is key to a good French knot. Just be sure not to hold it so tightly that the needle can't go back down through the fabric.

STRAIGHT STITCH (E) & LONG AND SHORT STITCH (F)

Straight stitches are clean and simple! This stitch is best used for outlines, but it is also effective as an accent when blending colors, adding texture, and more. Long and short stitch is worked the same way, just varying the length to have, well . . . long and short stitches.

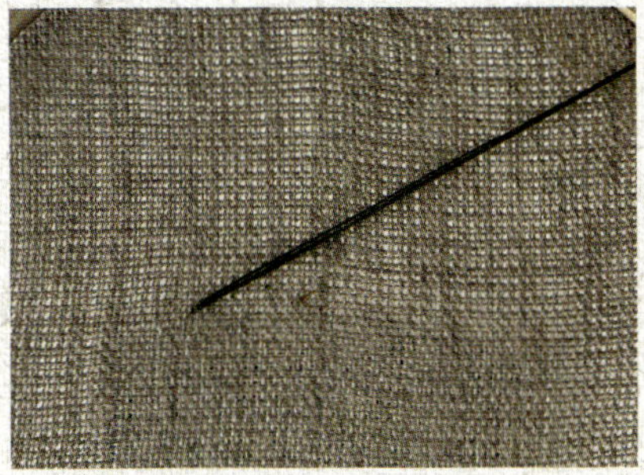

1. Go up until the knot stops the floss from going any farther.

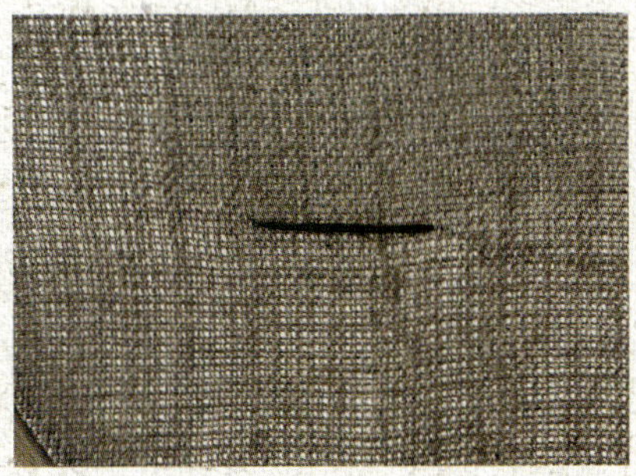

2. Go down through the fabric to the end of the line, following the pattern. This completes the straight stitch. Secure on back when finished.

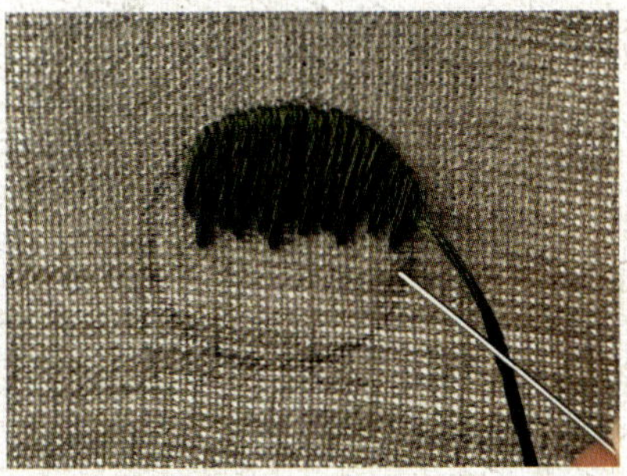

3. Varying straight stitches into longer and shorter lengths creates long and short stitches. Here, they're used to fill half of a circular area.

FISHBONE STITCH (G)

Fishbone stitch is great for making leaves!

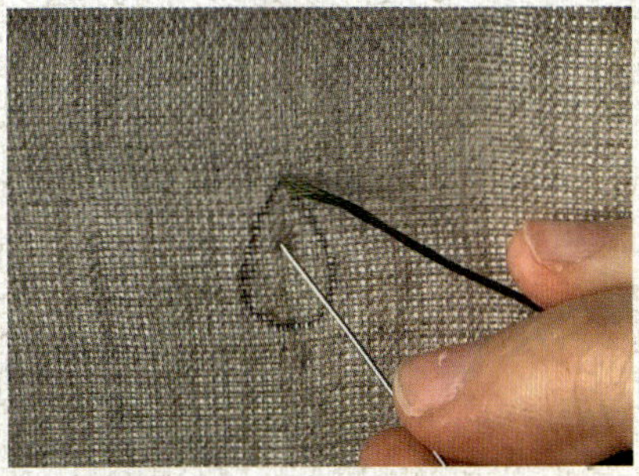

1. Start at the point of the leaf shape and make a small stitch along the middle line.

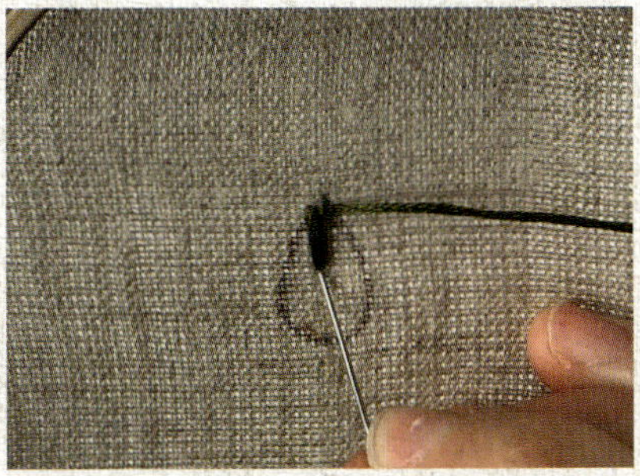

2. Go up a tiny bit lower than the first stitch on one side. Then, go down on the middle line slightly lower than the first stitch.

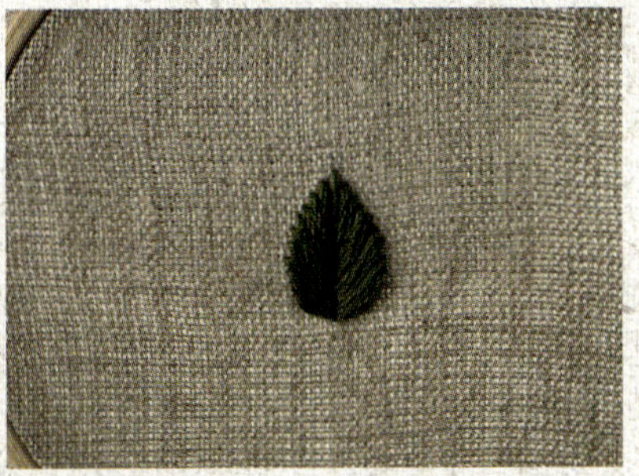

3. Repeat step 2 on the opposite side of the first stitch. Keep repeating from side to side until the stitches reach the bottom of the leaf. Secure on back when finished.

Tip Remember, after creating the first stich, your needle just needs to follow the shape of the outer lines and the center line while alternating sides.

LAZY DAISY STITCH (H)

Very similar to the chain stitch, the lazy daisy stitch is basically one chain repeated in a circle to create a small flower.

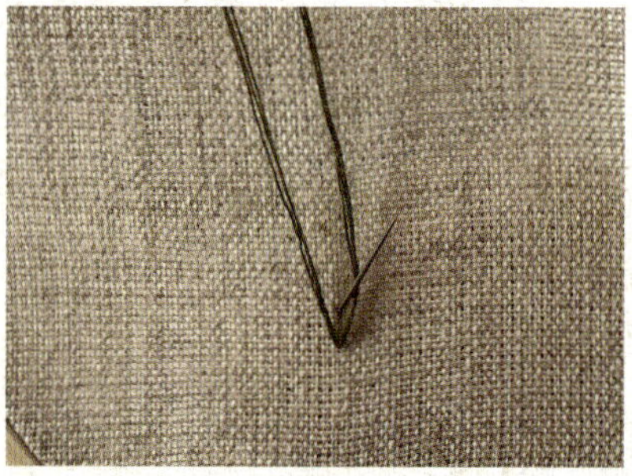

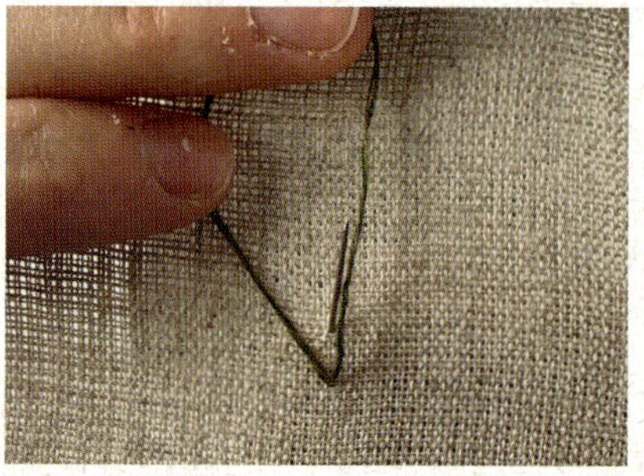

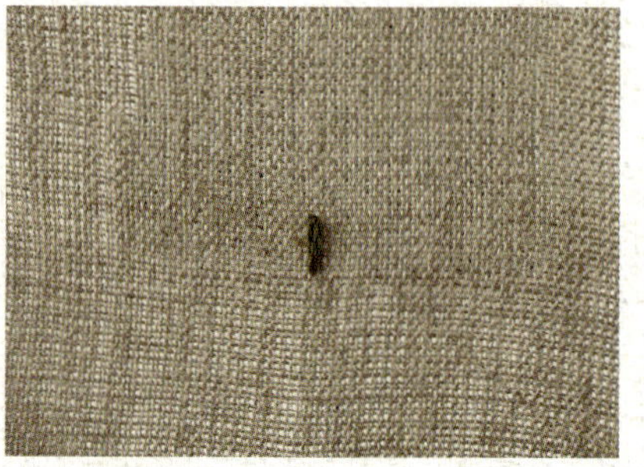

1. Go up until the knot stops the floss from going any farther. Go down through the same hole, but don't pull all the way through, creating a loop.
2. Thread the needle back up through the loop and pull tight.
3. Go down on the outside of the loop to secure it in place. Secure on back when finished. Once secured, this stitch looks like a single flower petal.

CHAIN STITCH (I)

Chain stitch works as a great filler or to make an extra-thick line.

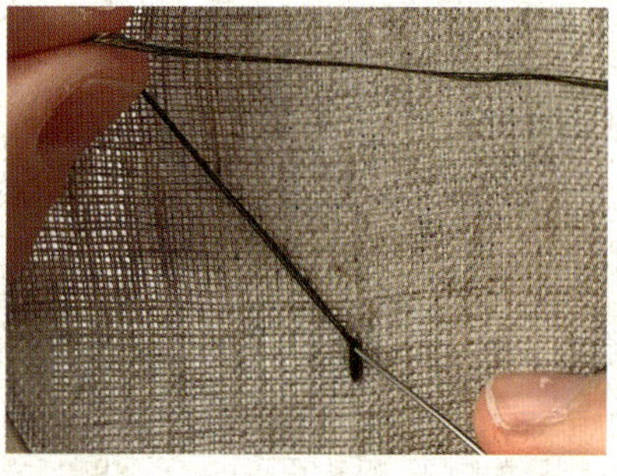

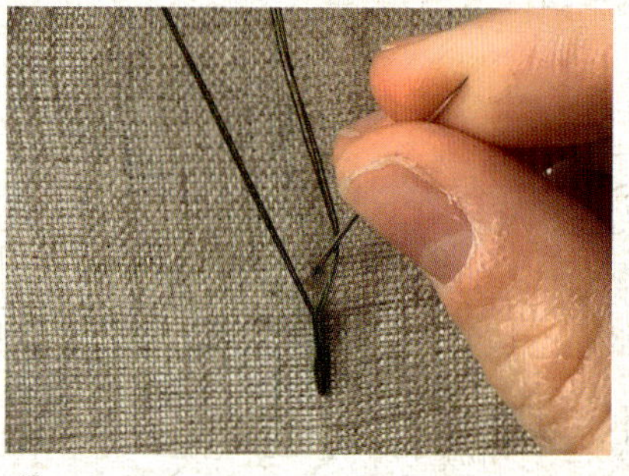

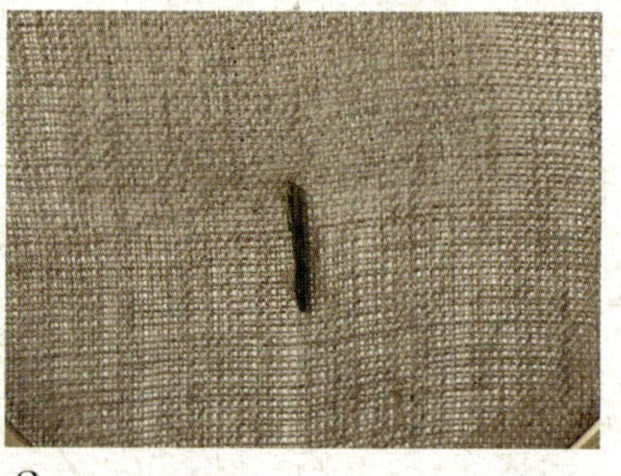

1. Follow steps 1 and 2 of lazy daisy stitch to create a loop, coming up through the loop. Go down through the hole the needle just created, but don't pull all the way through. This creates another loop on the front of the work.
2. Go up, coming through the loop about ¼" (.5 cm) away from the previous stitch, and pull all the way through. This secures the second loop.
3. To continue the chain, repeat steps 1 and 2. To finish, go down to lock the last loop in place. Secure on back when finished.

LOOPS (J)

Loops are great for adding accents to floral patterns, creating thick texture, or even creating leaves.

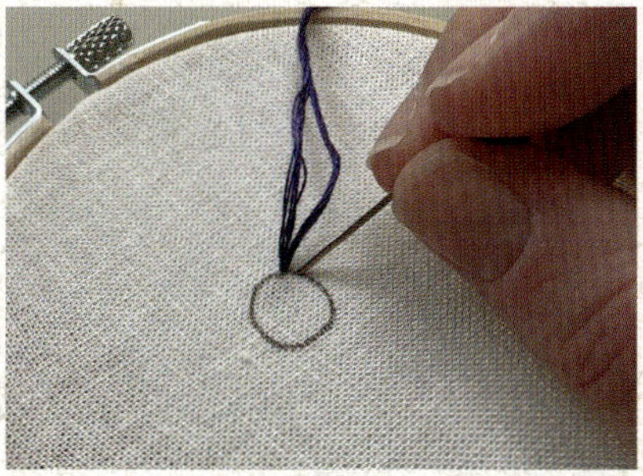

1. Go up until the knot stops the floss from going any farther. Carefully go back down close to where the needle came up, but don't pull all the way through, creating a loop.

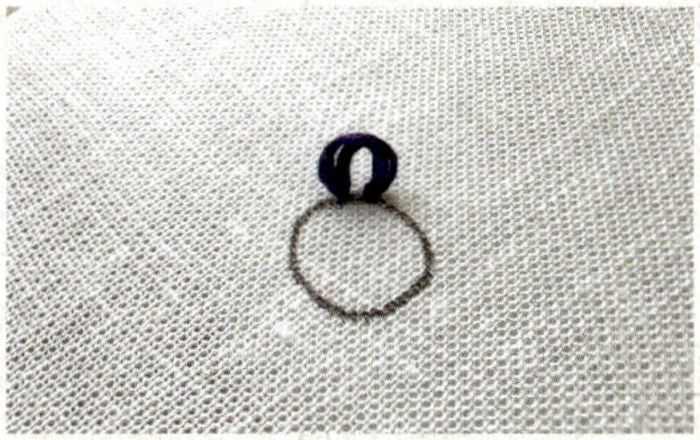

2. Keep doing this to fill the space. Secure on back when finished.

BLANKET STITCH

To skip the sewing machine for the bookmarks and eReader sleeve projects, blanket stitch is used to sew the fabric edges together.

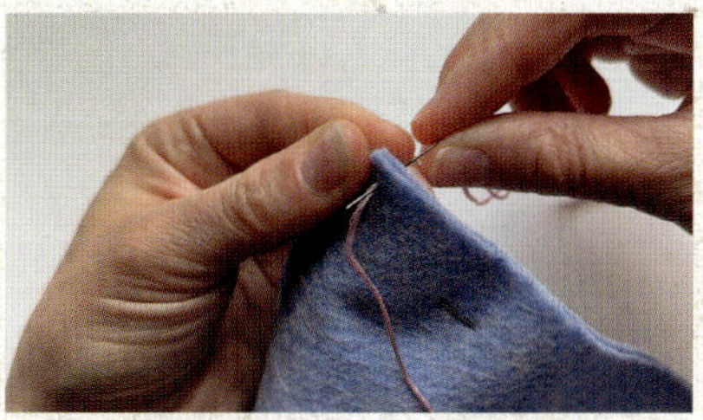

1. Begin by going up through your embroidered fabric piece about ¼" (.5 cm) from the edge. Then, layer your plain fabric behind the embroidered fabric. This "sandwiches" your knot between the layers. Wrap the thread to the back and pass the needle through both layers of felt, with your needle going from back to front and through the same hole.

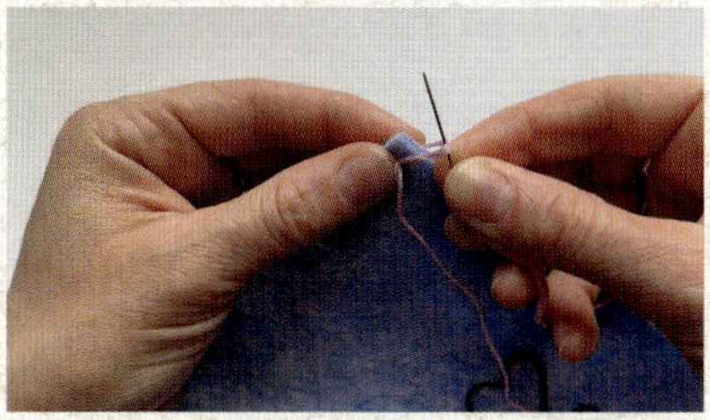

2. Before you pull the needle all the way through, leave a small length looping over the edge. Pass your needle through the loop and pull all the way to create your first stitch.

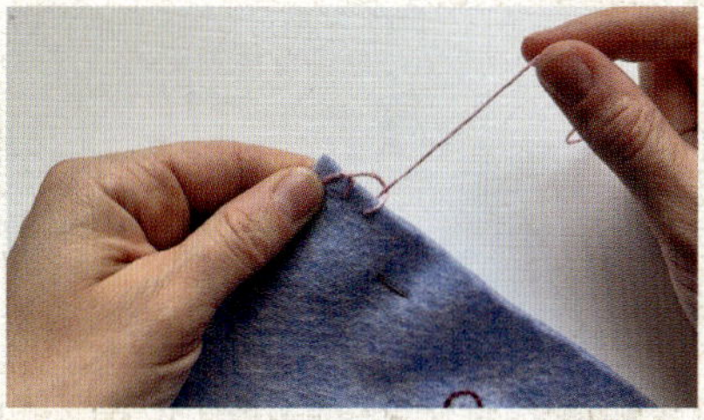

3. About ¼" (.5 cm) from the first stitch, go from front to back. Before pulling tight, pass the needle through the loop of thread.

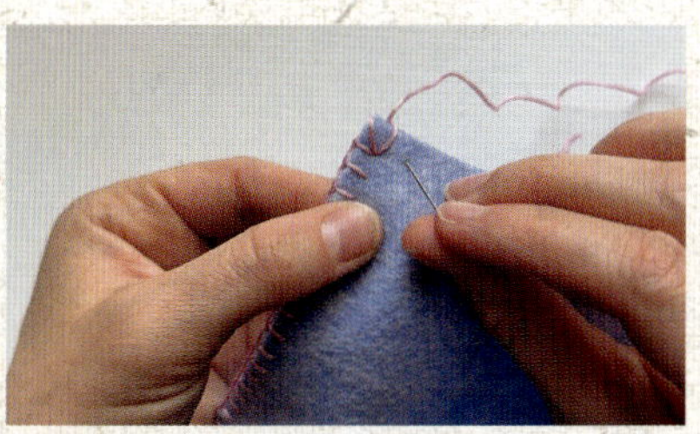

4. Repeat step 3 around the edge of the pieces you're stitching together. When you reach the end, secure with a knot to the inside of the project.

Beaded Embroidery

Adding beadwork to your embroidery doesn't have to be complicated! If you can do the backstitch, you can add beads and sequins. Depending on the size of the hole in your bead, you may need to use a fine beading needle.

ADDING SEED BEADS

As the name implies, seed beads are small seed-sized glass beads. The projects in this book use size 10 seed beads, but feel free to substitute what you can find in a color you like.

1. With a knot at one end of your floss, go up through the bottom of your fabric until the knot stops you. Then, thread on one seed bead until it touches your fabric.

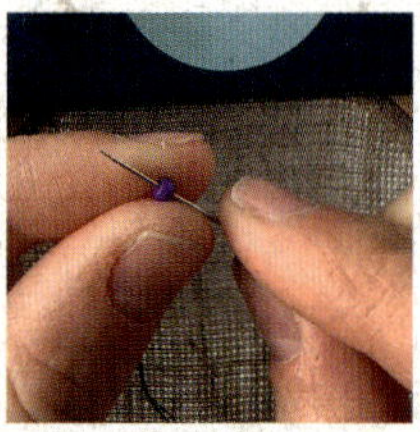

2. Go down through the fabric close to the bead. This secures the bead to the fabric. Repeat these steps, adding one bead with each additional stitch.

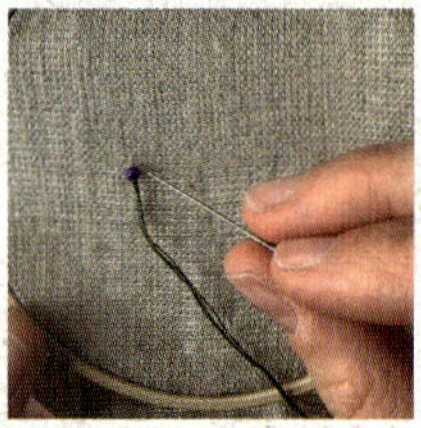

ADDING BUGLE BEADS

Bugle beads are small tubes with a hole running end to end. Their sizes range from as short as 2 mm to as long as 20 mm. The bugle beads used in The Dragon (p. 47) are 6 mm bugle beads. Add bugle beads using the same technique as seed beads. They look best stitched in unified rows for the greatest impact.

ADDING SEQUINS

Sequins are another way to add dimension and sparkle to your embroidery. The sequins you find at your local craft store will work well for embellishing. Look for options that are about 6–10 mm in size with a hole in the center.

1. With needle threaded, go up through the bottom of your fabric until the knot stops. Slide on one of your sequins onto the thread. Go back down through the fabric, next to where you came up.

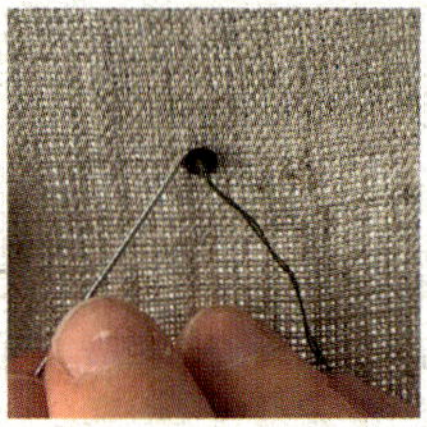

2. Come up about a sequin's distance away from the first. Slide another sequin on the needle. Then, go back down through the hole in the center of the previous sequin.

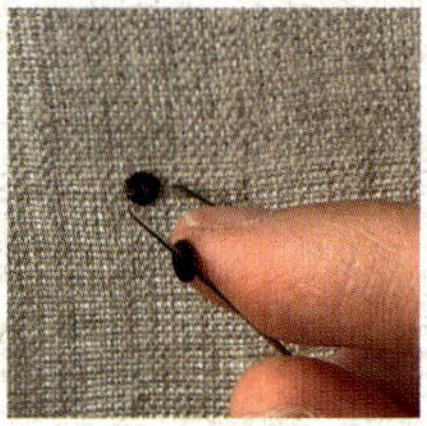

3. Repeat step 2 to add as many sequins as needed to fill a row or area.

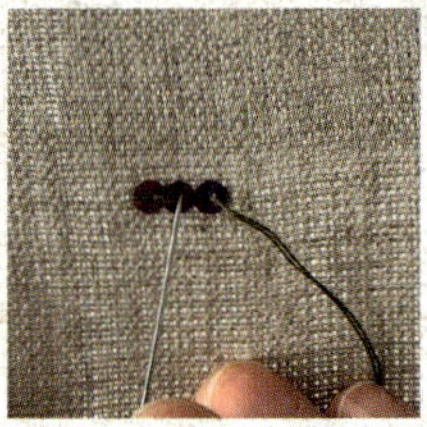

Finishing Your Work

There are many ways to finish an embroidery piece once the stitching is completed. Some people like to keep the design inside the working hoop, while others would rather frame it inside a classic photo frame or create an entirely new project out of it. Here is how to finish your work in the hoop.

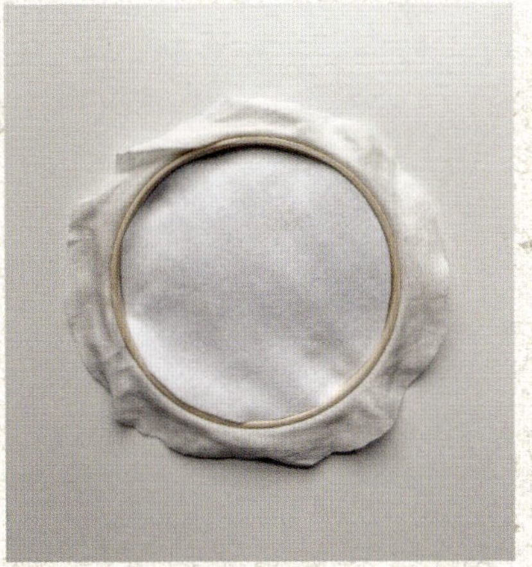

1. Cut a piece of felt to fit inside the back of the hoop and let it rest there between the hoops.

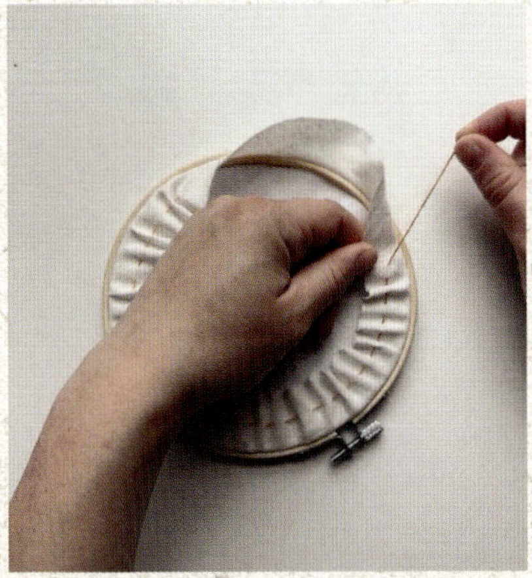

2. Cut a piece of floss and knot one end. Thread the floss through the fabric so the knot is covered by the excess fabric (the knot will be on the inside of the fabric). Weave the needle in and out (this back-and-forth stitch is called a *running stitch*) through all the excess fabric.

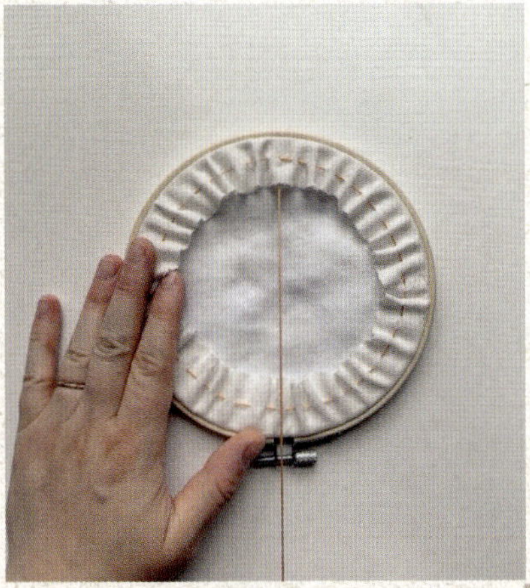

3. When you reach the beginning of your round, pull the thread tight to gather the fabric. Secure the floss in place with a knot and trim excess thread.

Tip

The tension of the running stitch through the excess fabric will hold the felt piece in place. This method is a less permanent way of finishing the hoop while making the back look clean.

How to Use This Book

The embroidery patterns in this book use an easy stitch-by-letter approach that tells you which stitch and color to use and where.

SUPPLIES, STITCHES, AND FLOSS

On the first page of each pattern, you'll find a complete list of supplies for that project. I've also provided a list of the stitches used in the embroidery with a letter in parentheses following each stitch. These letters relate to the stitch guide. The list of floss colors are what I used in the finished piece shown. Feel free to substitute these colors to suit your personal style!

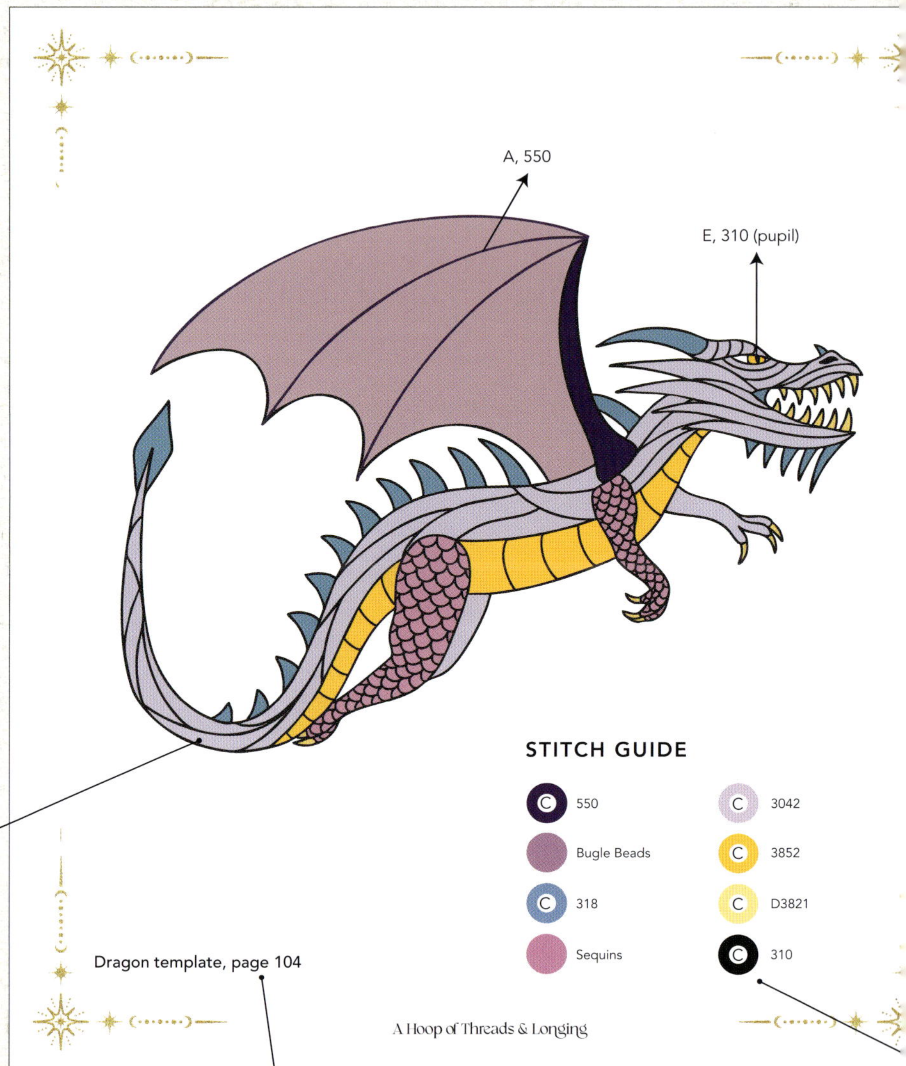

STITCH DIAGRAM

Each embroidery design has a full-color stitch diagram. You'll find each color also appears in the Stitch Guide.

TEMPLATE REFERENCE

This is the page where you'll find the traceable template to transfer your embroidery design to your fabric.

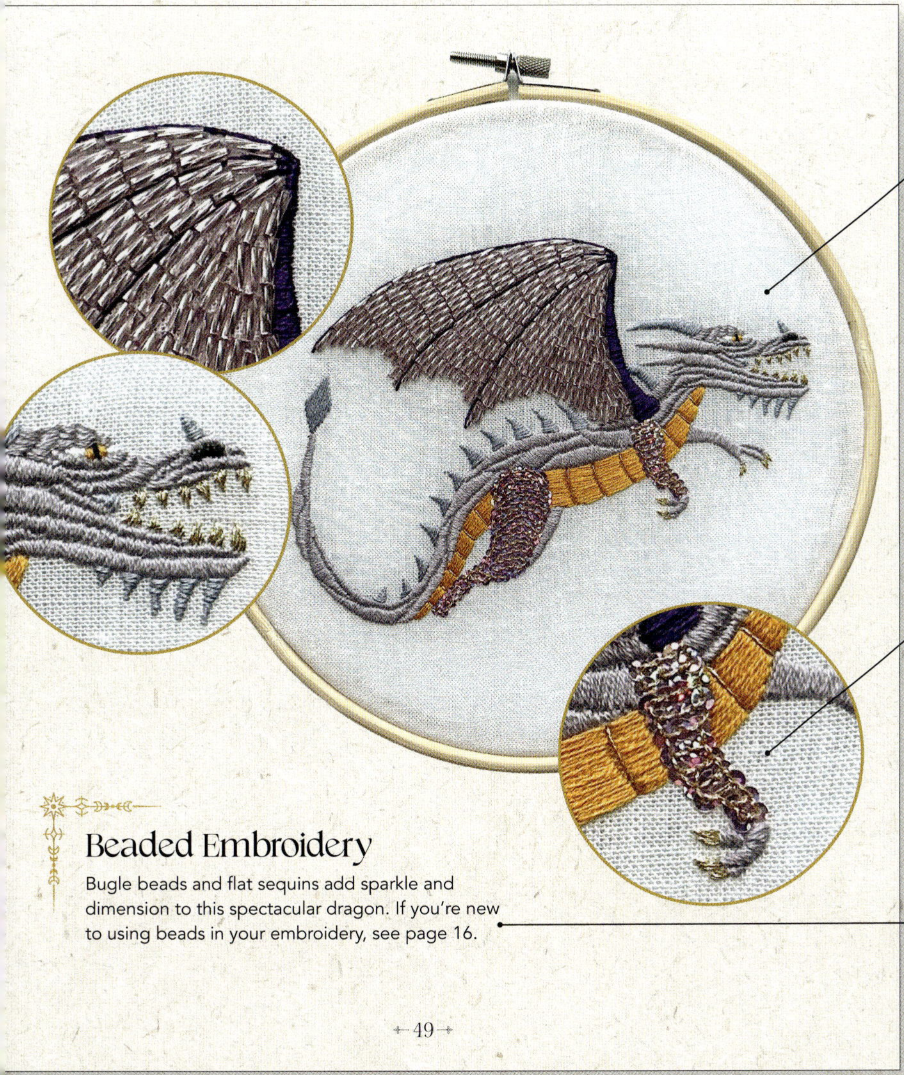
Beaded Embroidery

Bugle beads and flat sequins add sparkle and dimension to this spectacular dragon. If you're new to using beads in your embroidery, see page 16.

+ 49 +

FINISHED DESIGN

If you use the same colors and stitches as I did when making these projects, your finished design will look like mine!

DETAILS

Close up photos allow you to zoom in on important details.

TIPS

Many projects include helpful tips and tricks to make your stitching a breeze.

STITCH GUIDE

The Stitch Guide acts as your key to knowing which stitches and colors to use. For example, a purple circle with the letter C and number 158 after it means you fill the purple areas with satin stitch using DMC 550. Occasionally, the same color is used for two different stitches. When this happens, an arrow pointing to an extra stitch and color label will highlight that section.

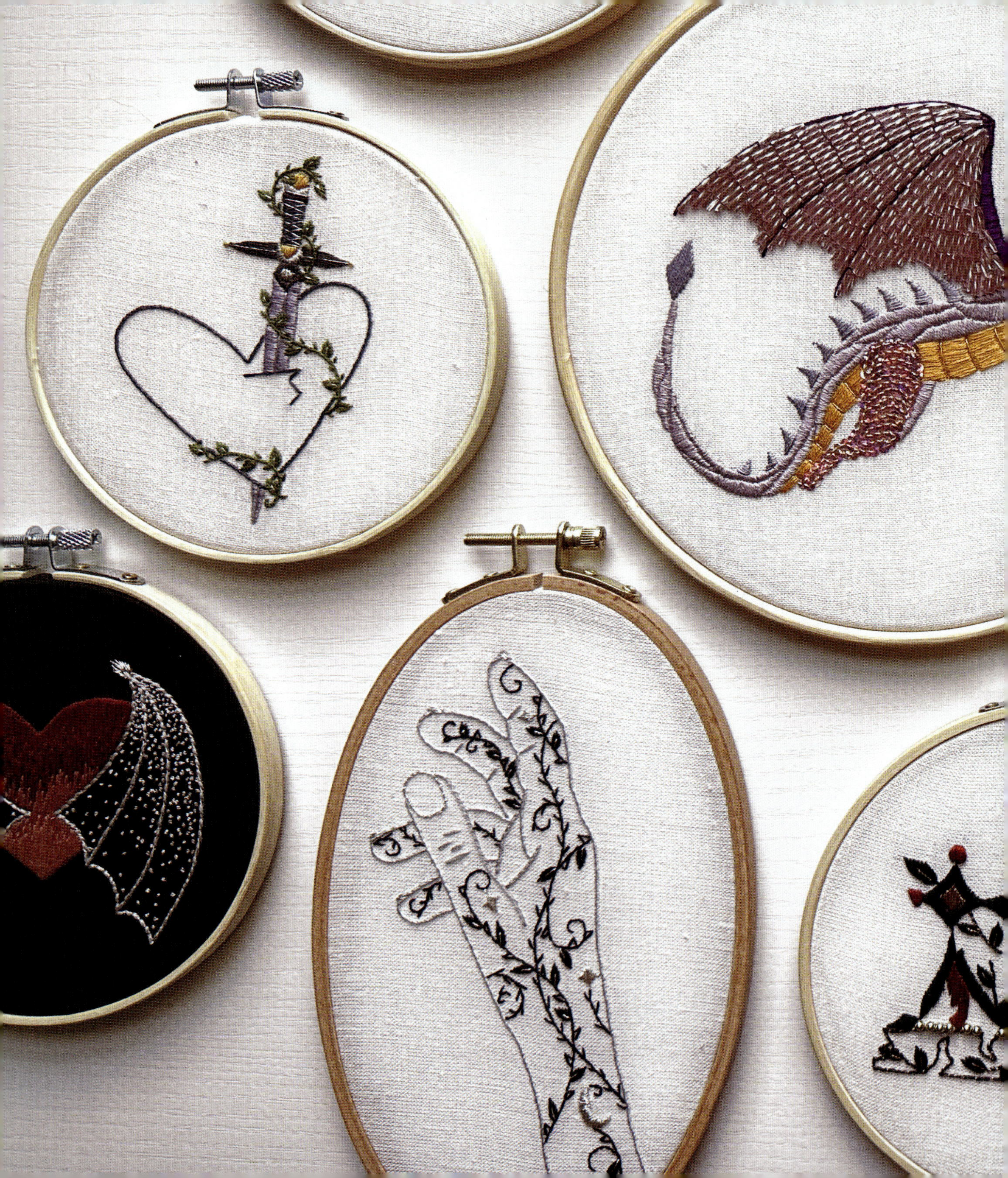

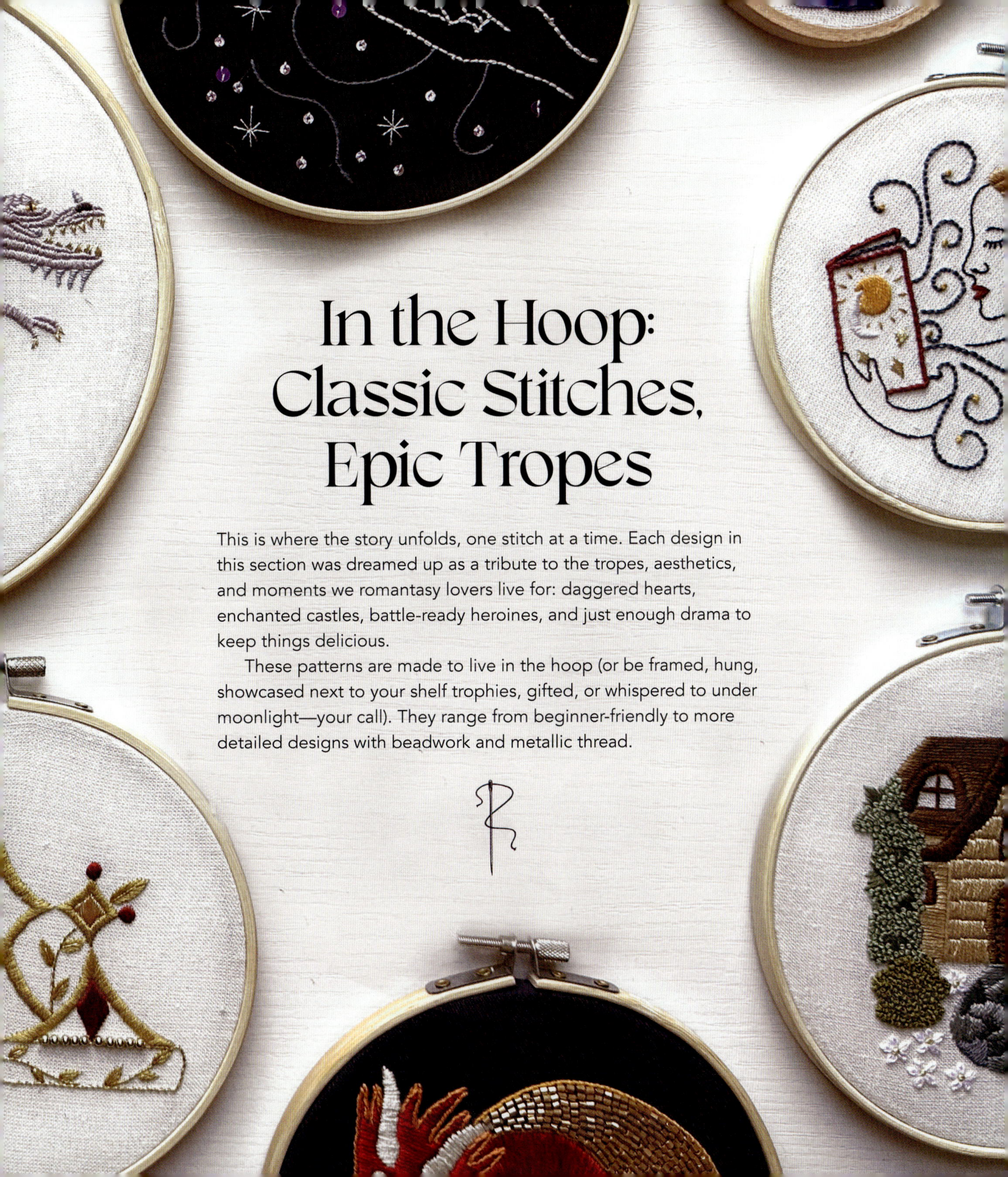

In the Hoop: Classic Stitches, Epic Tropes

This is where the story unfolds, one stitch at a time. Each design in this section was dreamed up as a tribute to the tropes, aesthetics, and moments we romantasy lovers live for: daggered hearts, enchanted castles, battle-ready heroines, and just enough drama to keep things delicious.

These patterns are made to live in the hoop (or be framed, hung, showcased next to your shelf trophies, gifted, or whispered to under moonlight—your call). They range from beginner-friendly to more detailed designs with beadwork and metallic thread.

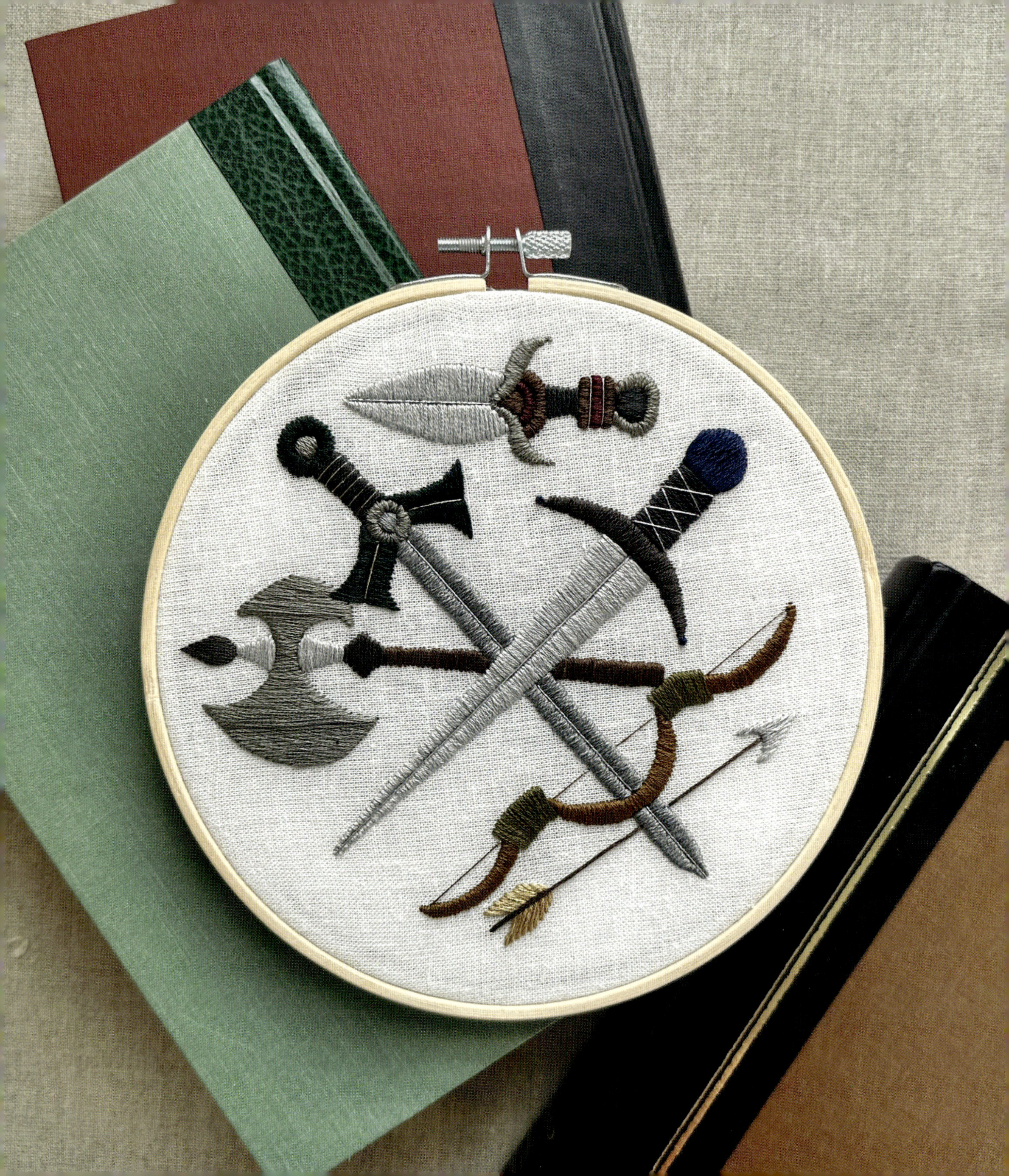

Self-Rescuing Princess

She's not waiting for a knight. This fierce design celebrates the self-rescuing princess. She is well prepared with a full stash of battle knives, daggers, pointy fierce things, and serious main character energy.

SUPPLIES

7" (18 cm) Embroidery Hoop

Fabric

Fabric Scissors

Embroidery Needle

Embroidery Scissors

STITCHES

Satin Stitch (C): page 12

Straight Stitch (E): page 13

THREADS

DMC Floss Colors

168	869
169	3011
336	3799
464	3802
500	D168
646	D3801
839	D3821
844	

Note

Use six strands of floss throughout, except for D168, D3801, and D3821, use one strand.

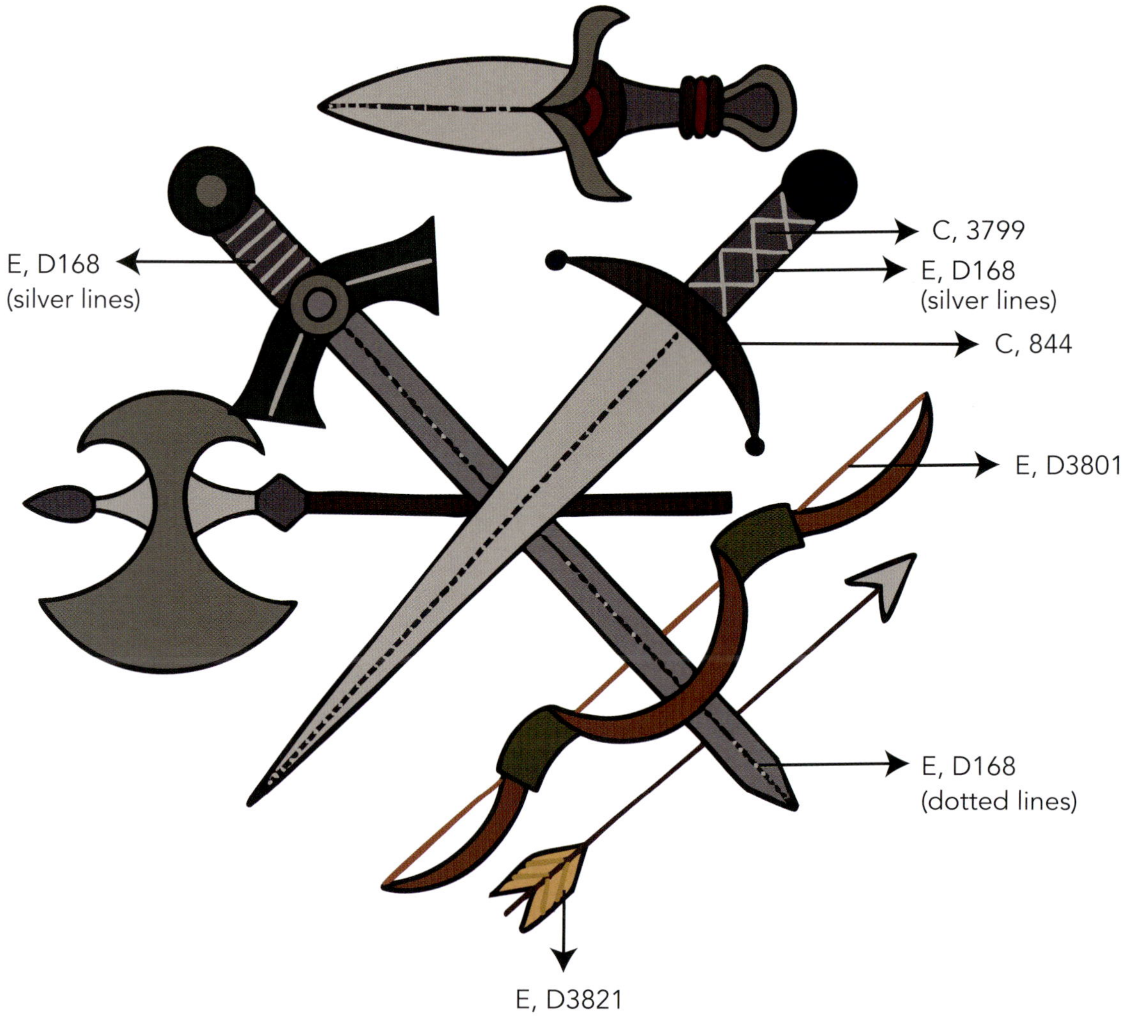

STITCH GUIDE

C 168	C 336	C 464	C 646
C 169	C 869	C 3011	C 3802
C 3799	C 839	C 500	

Weapons template, page 108

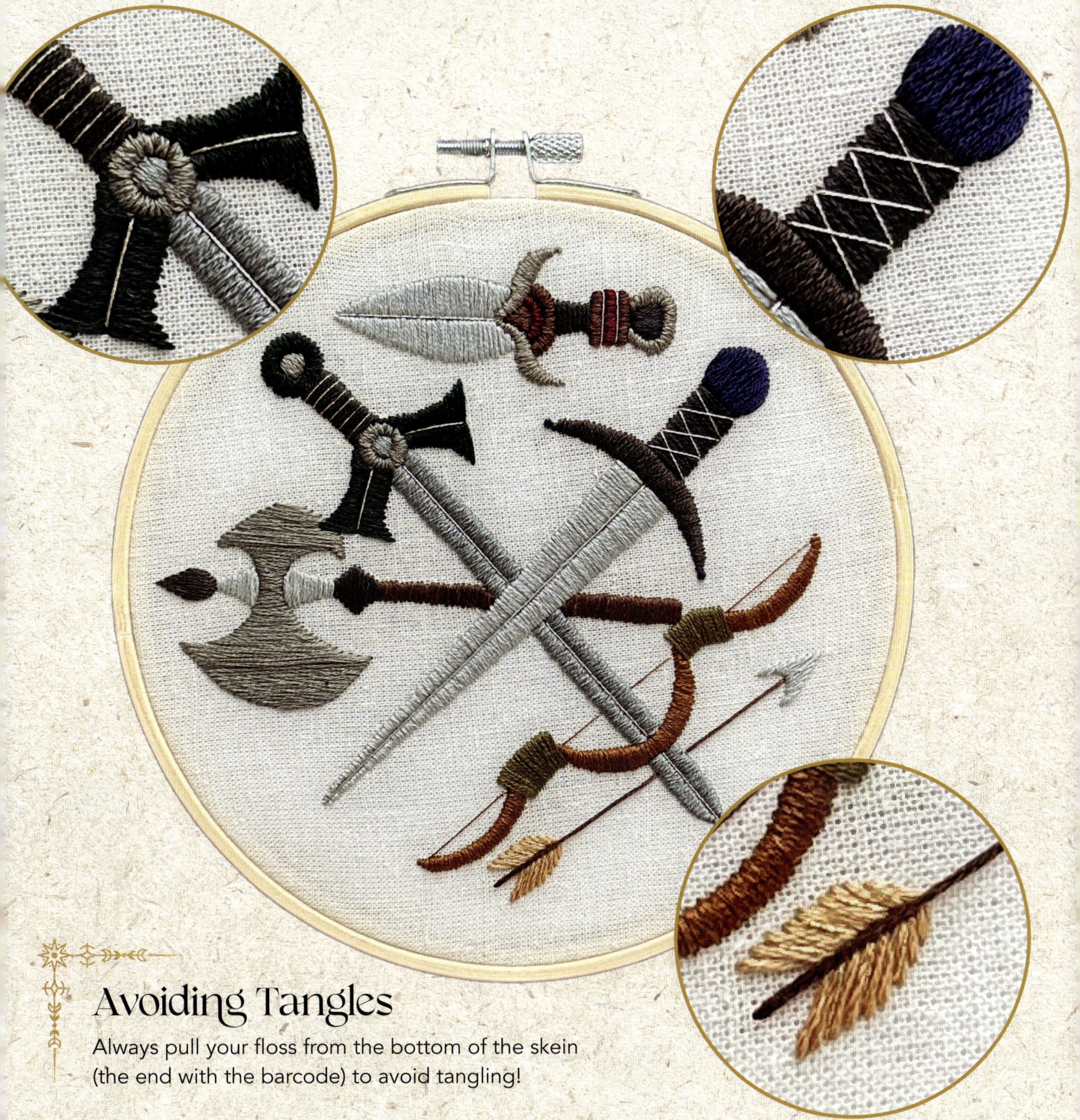

Avoiding Tangles

Always pull your floss from the bottom of the skein (the end with the barcode) to avoid tangling!

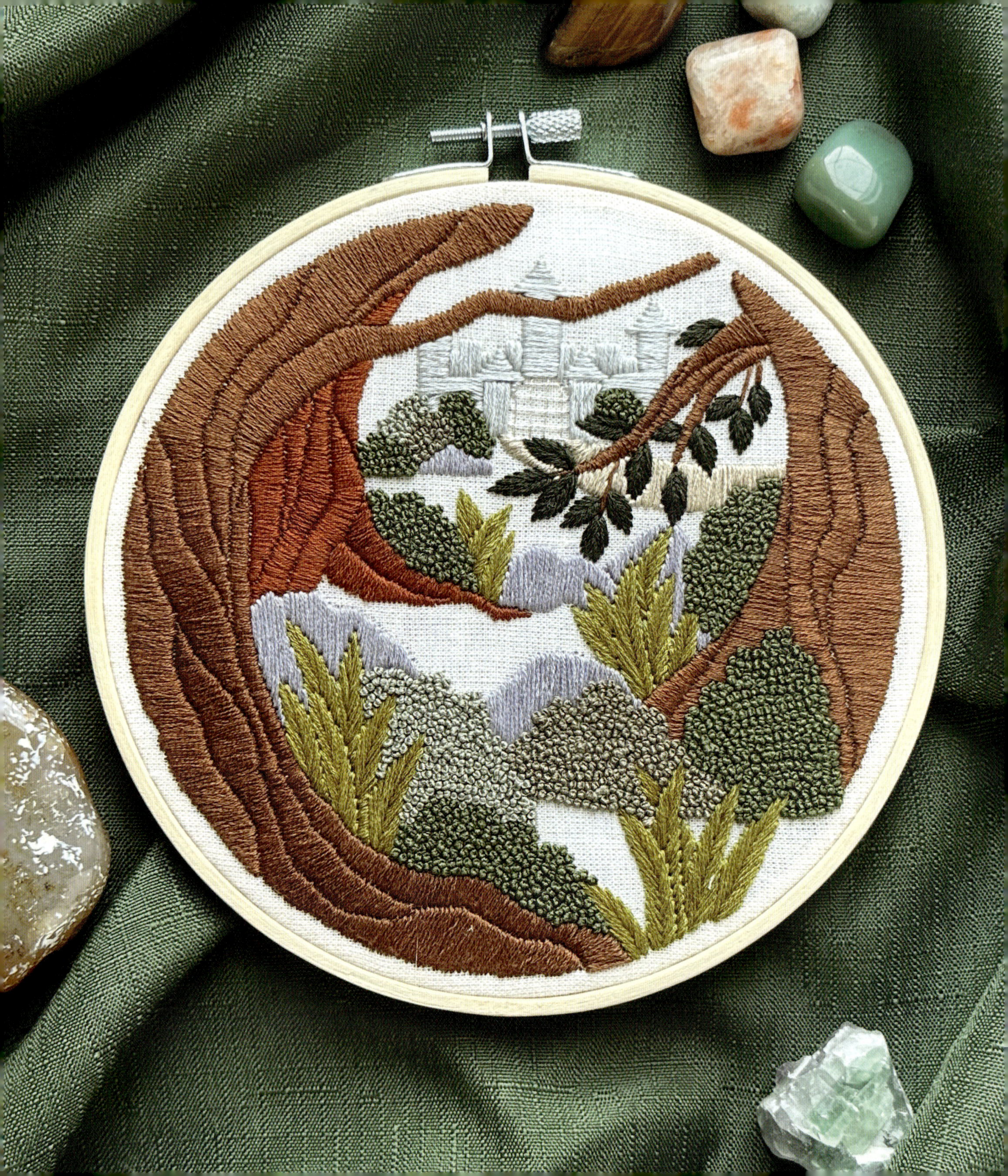

Road to the Castle

Every epic starts with a journey. This winding path leads to a distant castle, capturing the anticipation, mystery, and heartbreak of a quest. Stitch it in muted tones for a misty vibe, or go bold with twilight blues and golds—your journey, your palette.

SUPPLIES

7" (18 cm) Embroidery Hoop

Fabric

Fabric Scissors

Embroidery Needle

Embroidery Scissors

STITCHES

Satin Stitch (C): page 12

French Knots (D): page 12

Straight Stitch (E): page 13

Fishbone Stitch (G): page 13

THREADS

DMC Floss Colors

168	934
300	3022
318	3051
640	3782
731	D168
801	

Note

Use six strands of floss throughout, except for D168, use one strand.

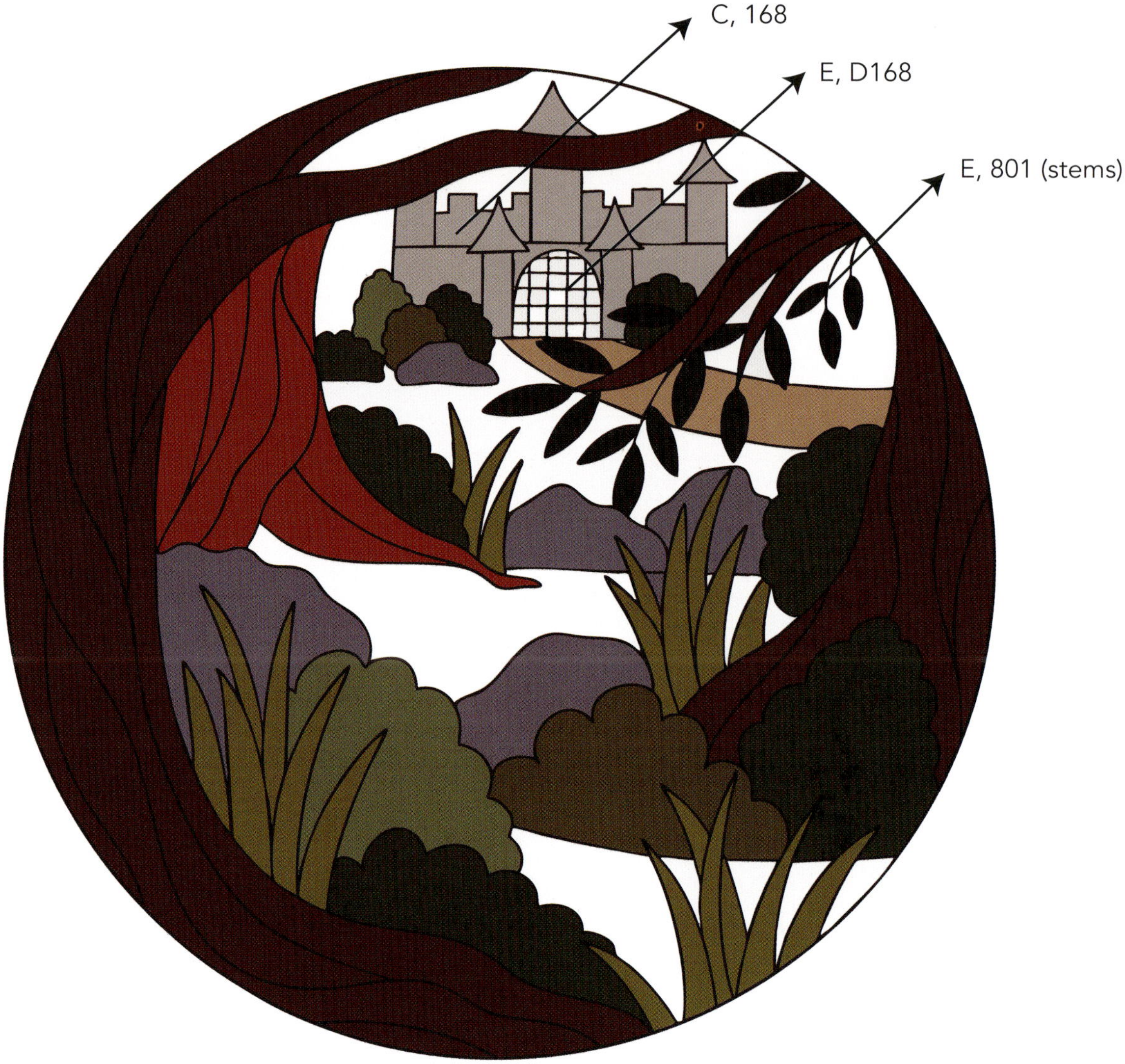

STITCH GUIDE

C 801	C 168	D 3051	C 3782
C 300	G 934	D 3022	
C 318	G 731	D 640	

Castle template, page 108

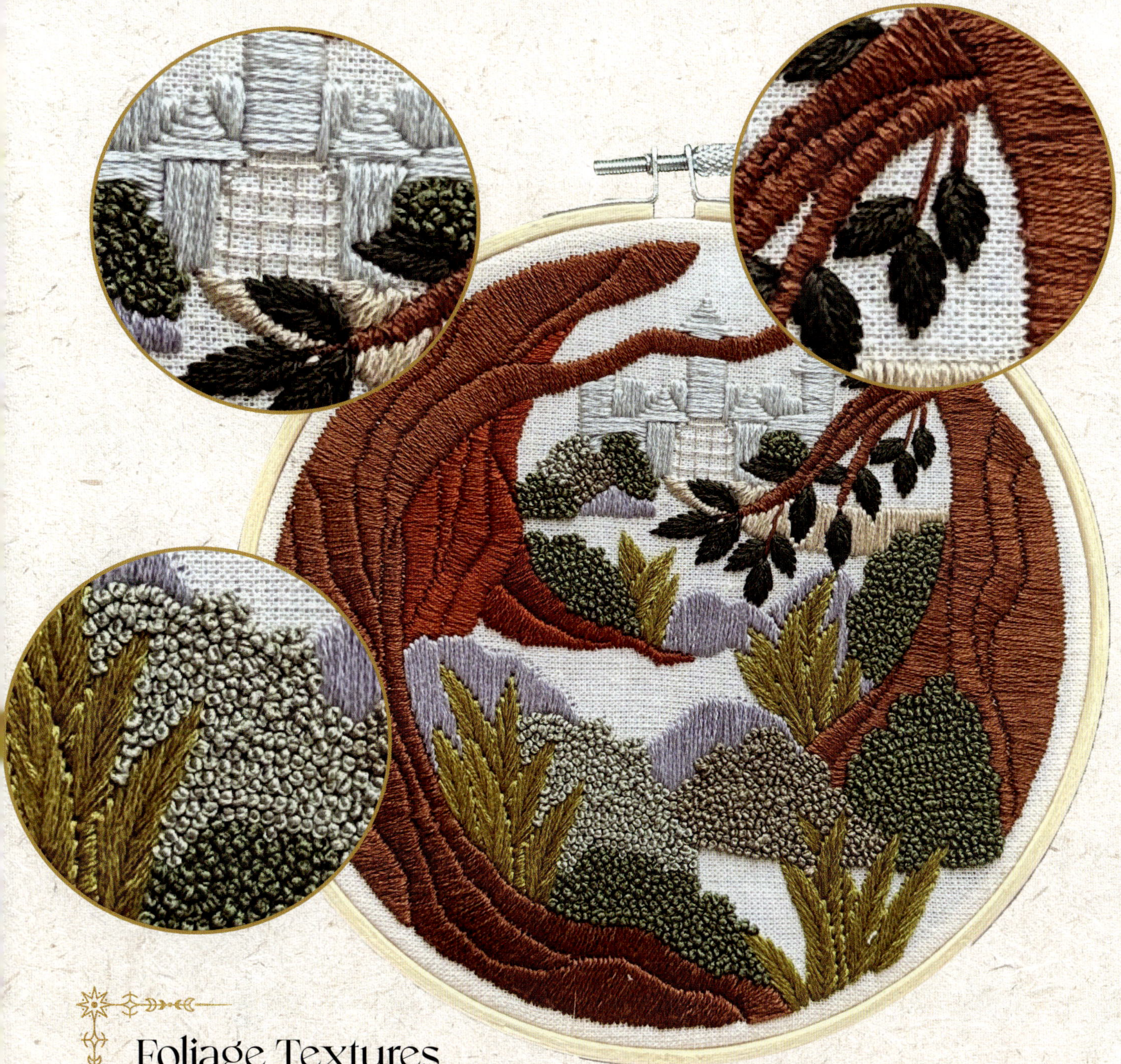

Foliage Textures

Densely packing French knots gives the illusion of moss and bushes growing in the forest. Pair these stitches with fishbone stitch for ferns and satin stitch for rocks, and you've made a magical scene.

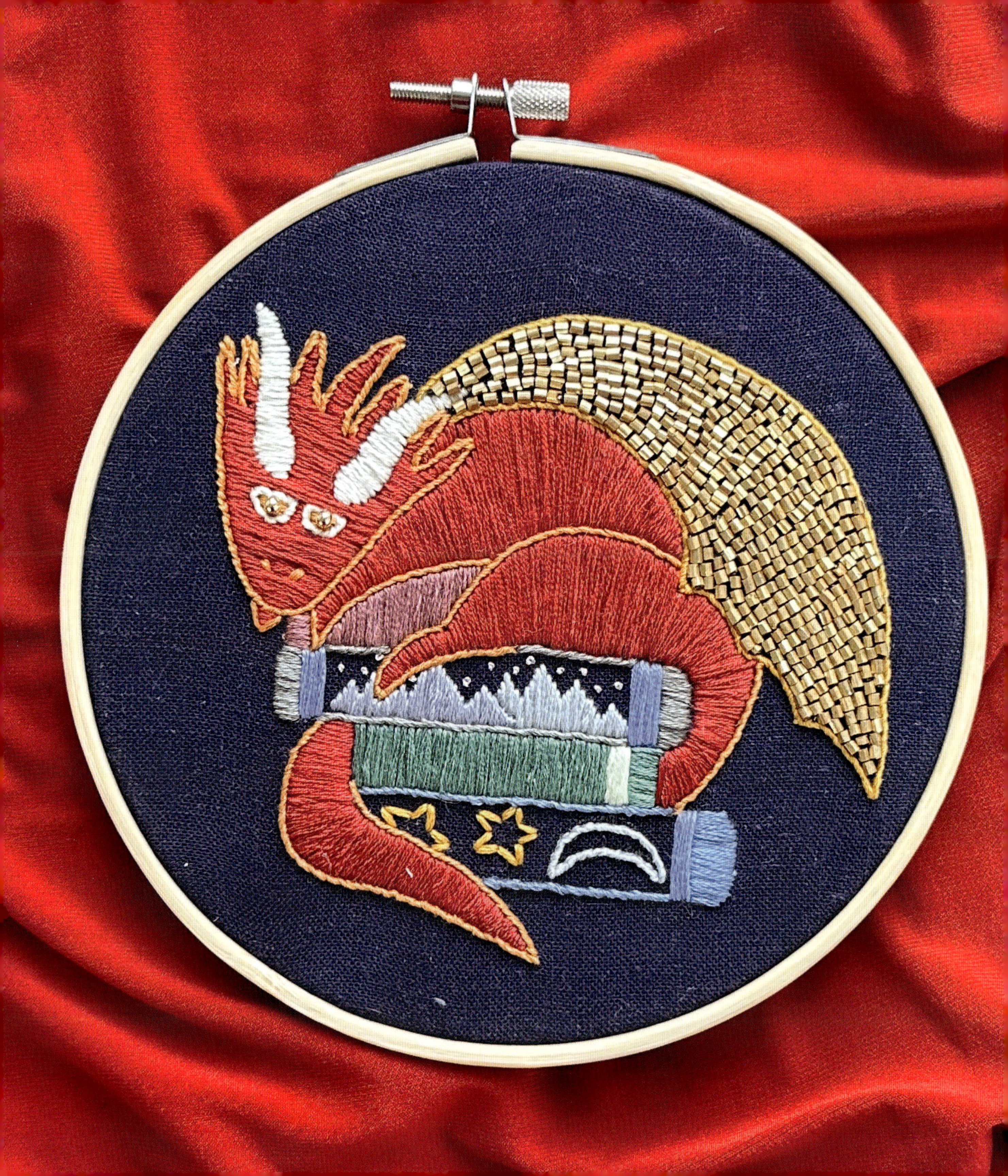

Book Dragon's Hoard

This dragon isn't guarding gold—he's curled around a hoard of books. With shimmering thread and soft curves, he's the ultimate cozy guardian of your library. And no, he's *not* a hoarder—he's a collector. Big difference. Especially when it comes to special editions.

SUPPLIES

6" (15 cm) Embroidery Hoop

Fabric

Fabric Scissors

Embroidery Needle

Embroidery Scissors

Fine Beading Needle (or small embroidery needle)

2 mm Gold Bugle Beads

2 Gold Seed Beads (for eyes)

STITCHES

Whipped Backstitch (A): page 11

Satin Stitch (C): page 12

French Knots (D): page 12

Straight Stitch (E): page 13

THREADS

DMC Floss Colors

163	931
168	976
498	3726
646	3839
746	3852
772	D168

Note

Use six strands of floss throughout, except for D168, use one strand.

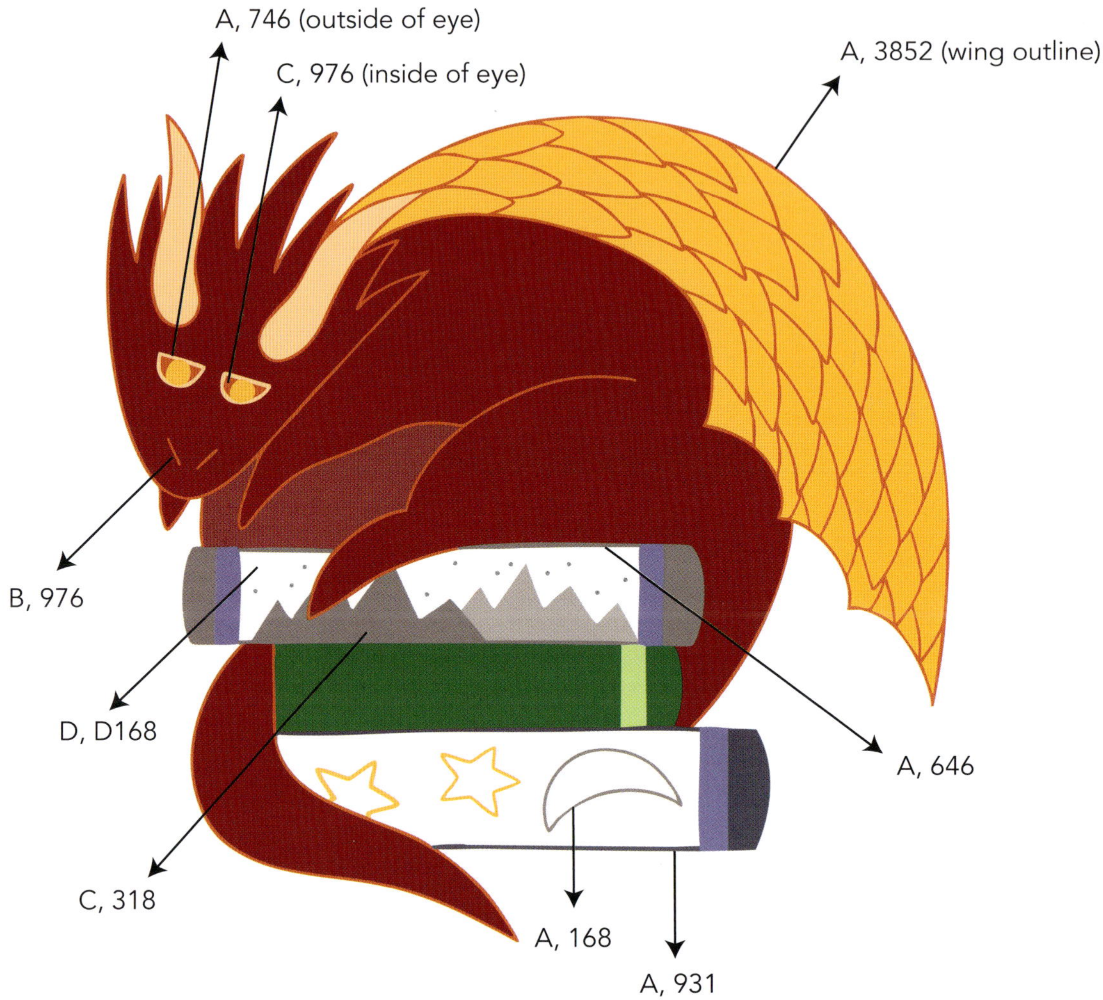

STITCH GUIDE

C 498	E 3852	C 772	C 646
C 3726	C 746	C 931	C 168
A 976	C 163	C 3839	Gold Beads

Dragon and Books template, page 105

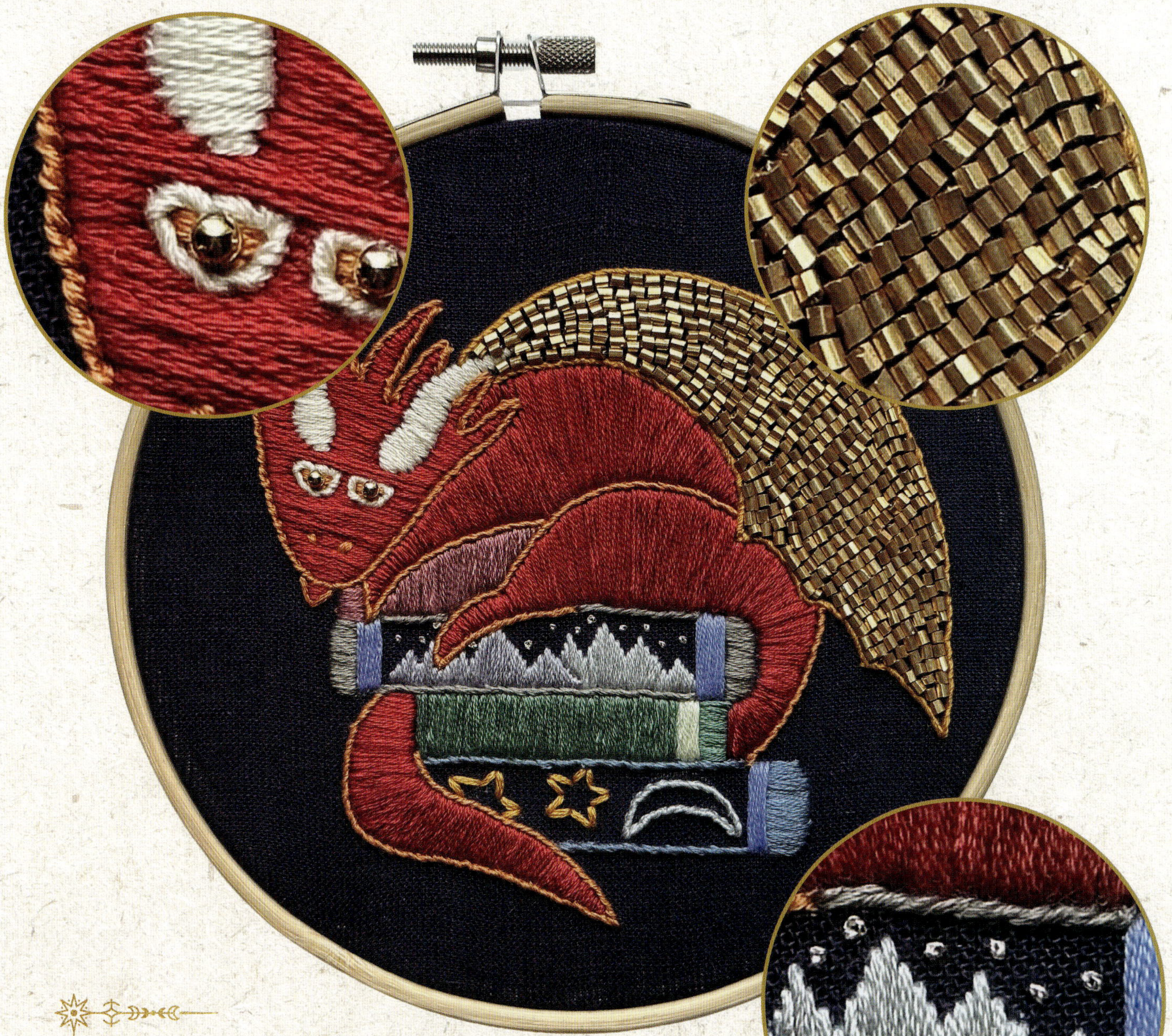

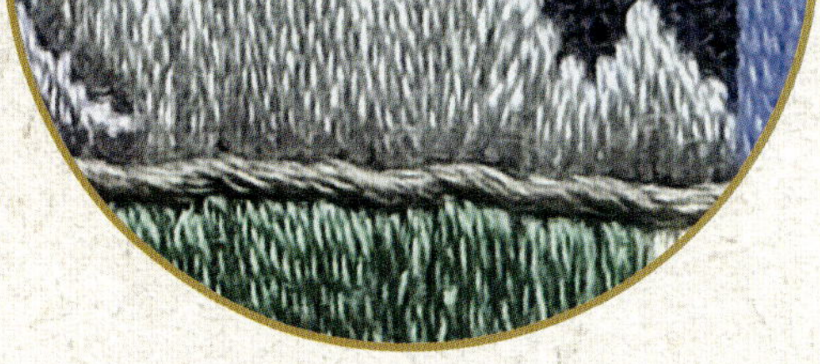

Beaded Embroidery

The gold beads used in this dragon's wings add sparkle and dimension. If you're new to using beads in your embroidery, see page 16.

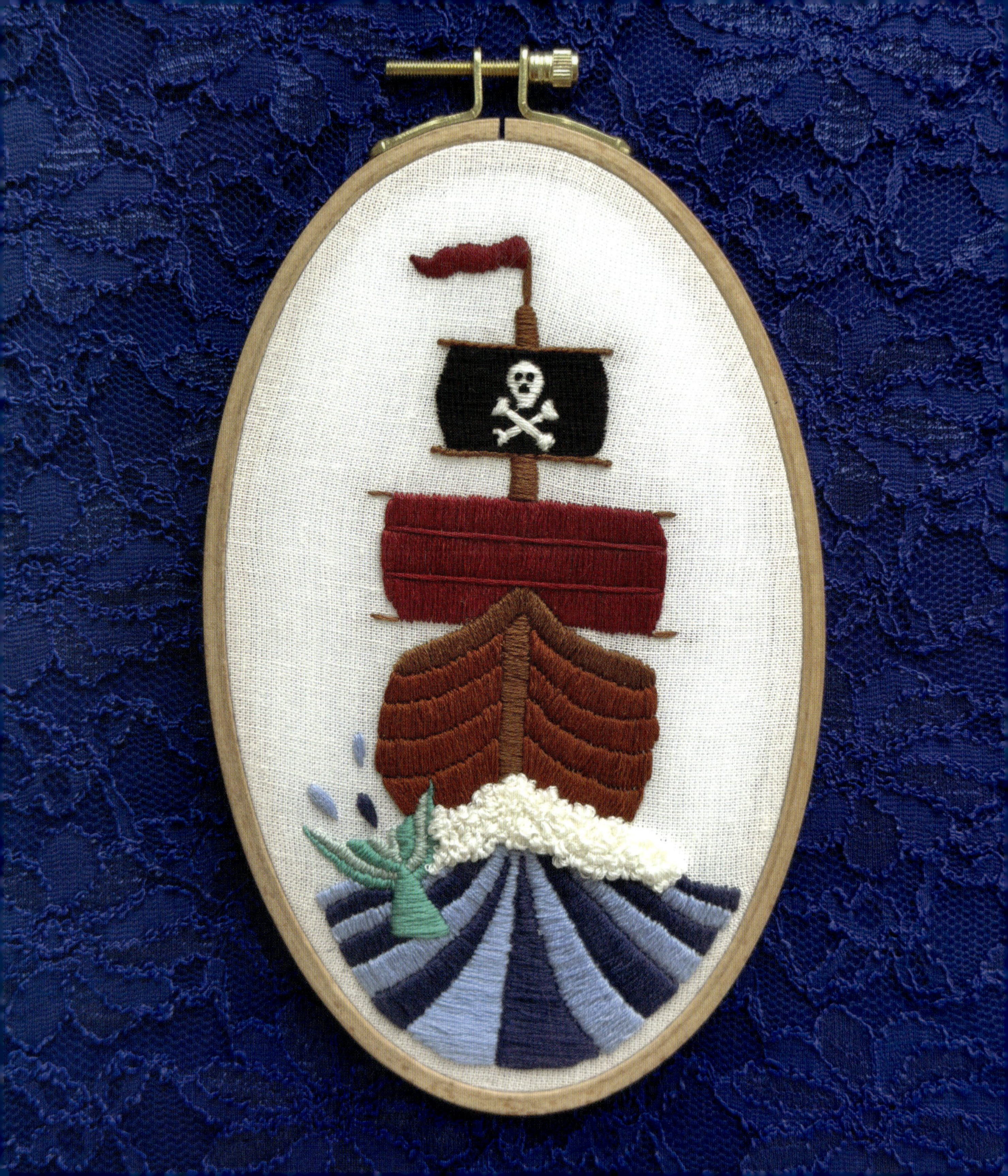

Sirens & Sails

Oh! A pirate's love and a ship on the edge of enchantment. This design hints at a tale of pirates and the sirens they can't resist. It's a story on the cusp of something magical … and maybe a little dangerous.

SUPPLIES

8 × 5" (20 × 13 cm) Oval Embroidery Hoop

Fabric

Fabric Scissors

Embroidery Needle

Embroidery Scissors

STITCHES

Whipped Backstitch (A): page 11

Satin Stitch (C): page 12

French Knots (D): page 12

Straight Stitch (E): page 13

Loops (J): page 15

THREADS

DMC Floss Colors

300	814
310	958
334	3813
336	3865
801	

Note

Use six strands of floss throughout, except for the black flag. For the flag, use three strands.

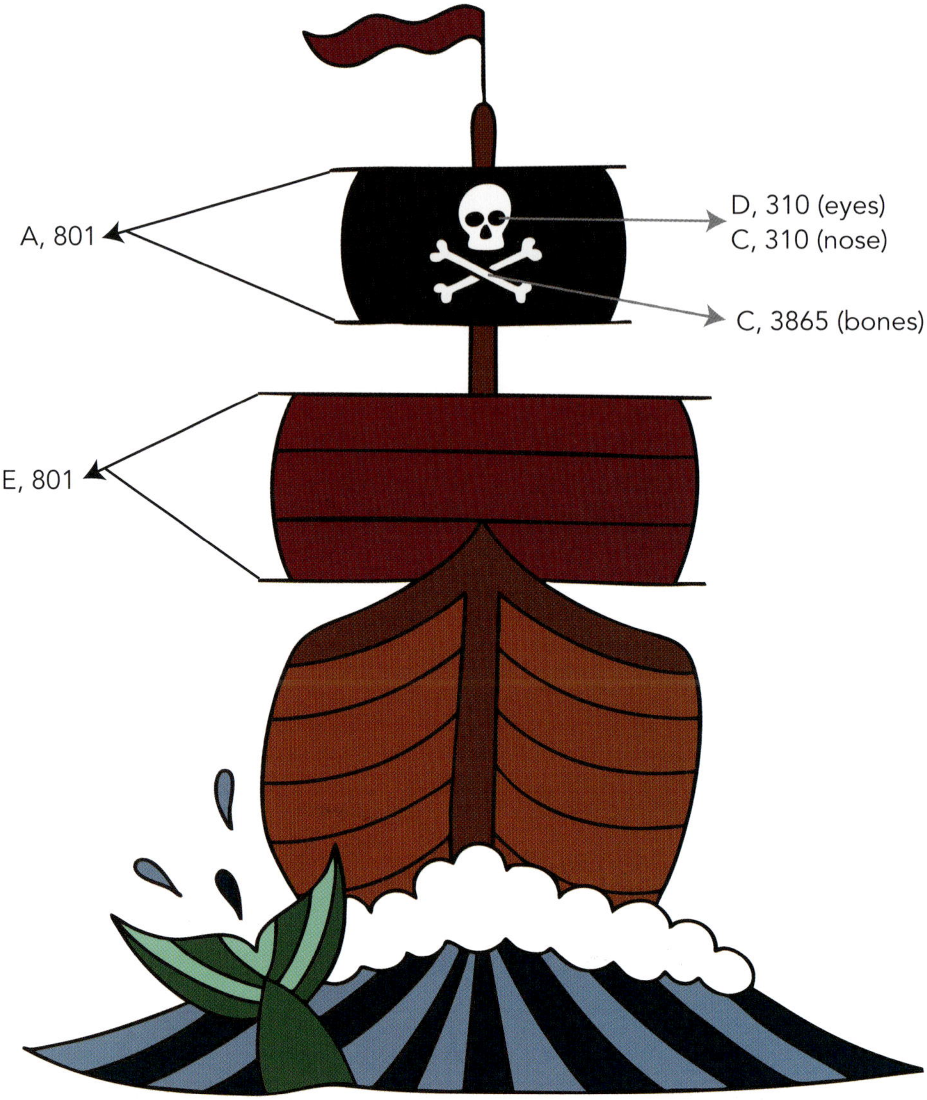

STITCH GUIDE

C 336	C 814	C 3813
C 334	C 801	C 310
C 300	C 958	J 3865 (12 strands)

Pirate Ship template, page 106

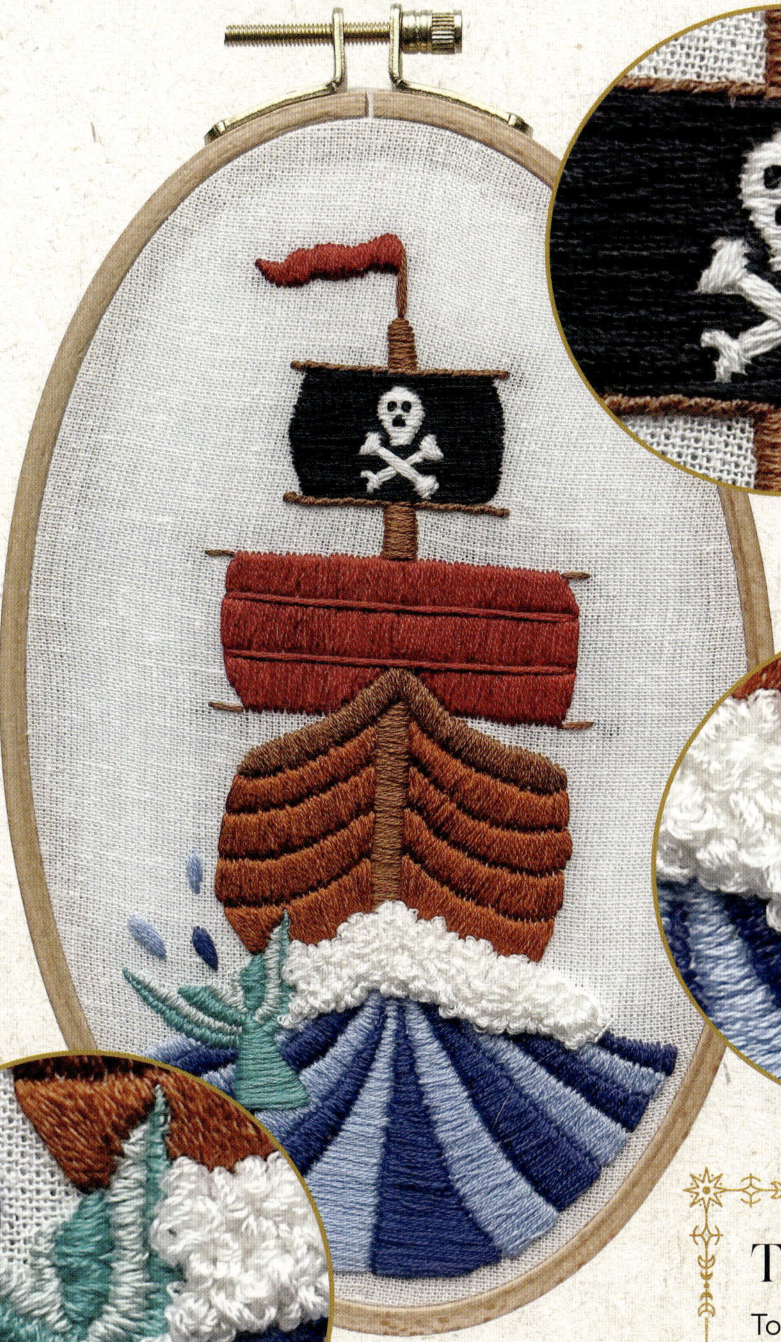

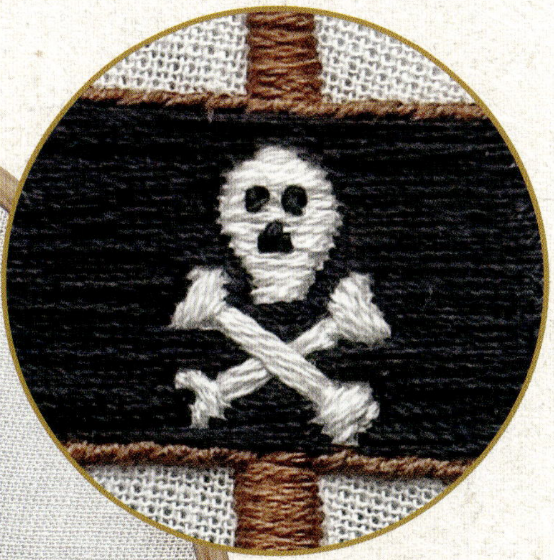

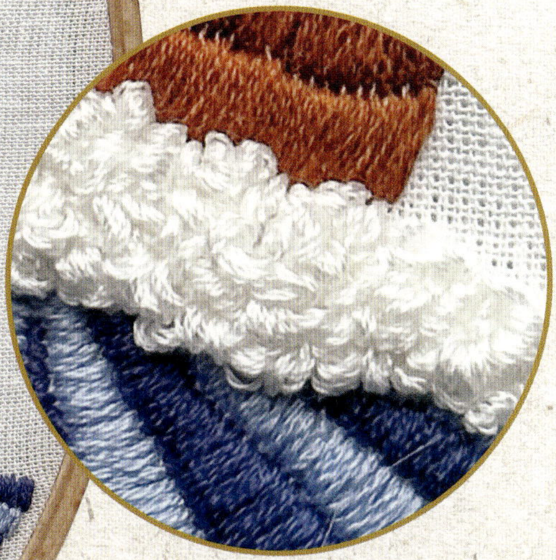

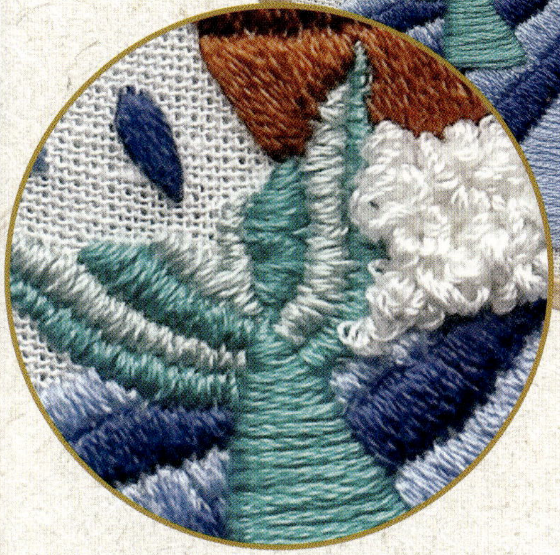

Twelve Stands

To thread 12 strands, simply pull the threads all the way through, as you would for six strands, until the ends meet. Tie the two ends together to form a knot.

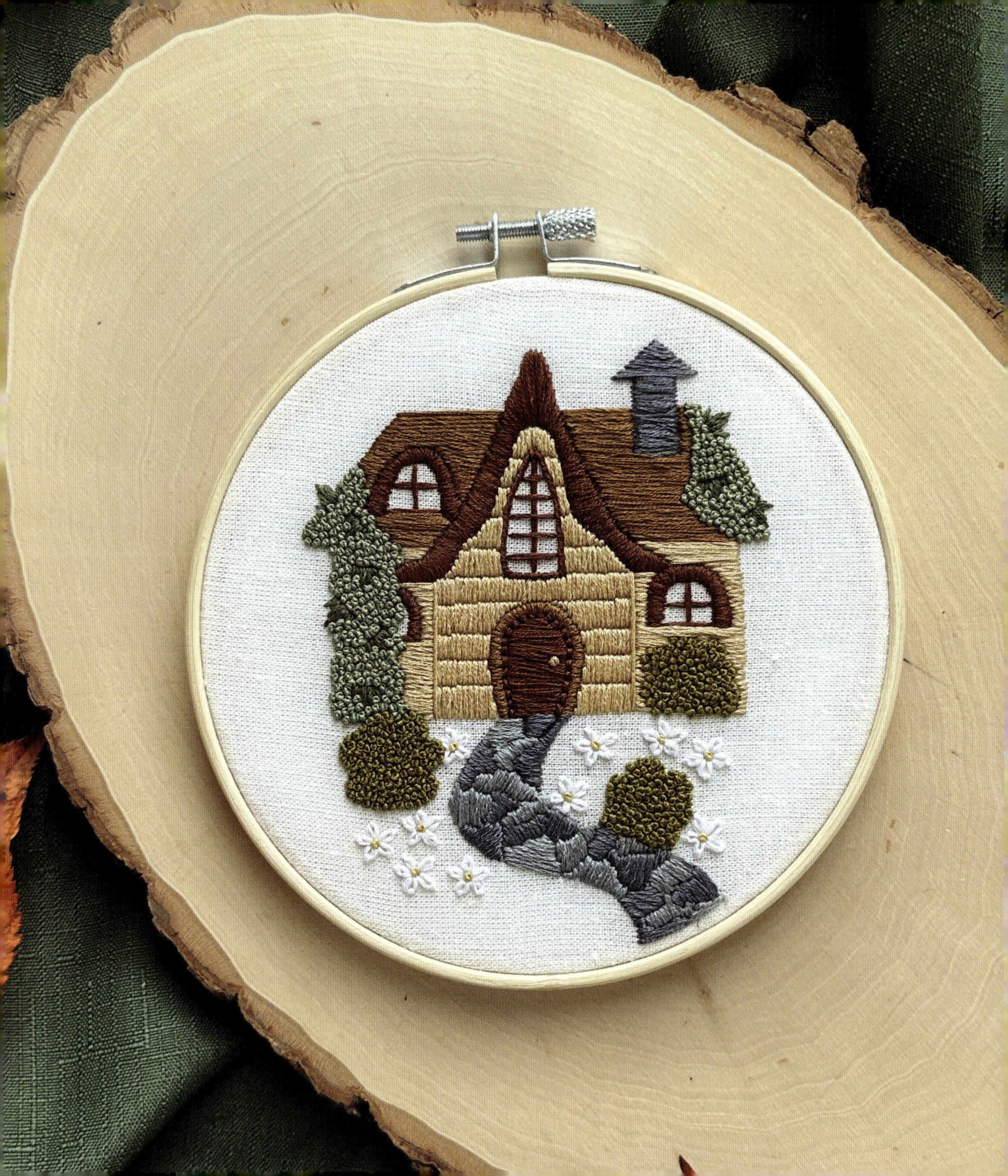

Cottagecore Romance

Think quiet woods, warm bread, and the kind of love that blooms with the seasons. This pattern is all soft vines, cozy windows, and gentle magic—perfect for fans of the slow life and sweet kisses by the fire. Stitch it with love (and maybe a few wildflowers).

SUPPLIES

6" (15 cm) Embroidery Hoop

Fabric

Fabric Scissors

Embroidery Needle

Embroidery Scissors

STITCHES

Whipped Backstitch (A): page 11

Satin Stitch (C): page 12

French Knots (D): page 12

Straight Stitch (E): page 13

Lazy Daisy Stitch (H): page 14

THREADS

DMC Floss Colors

169	869
317	3051
422	3052
731	3822
801	B5200
839	

Note

Use six strands of floss throughout.

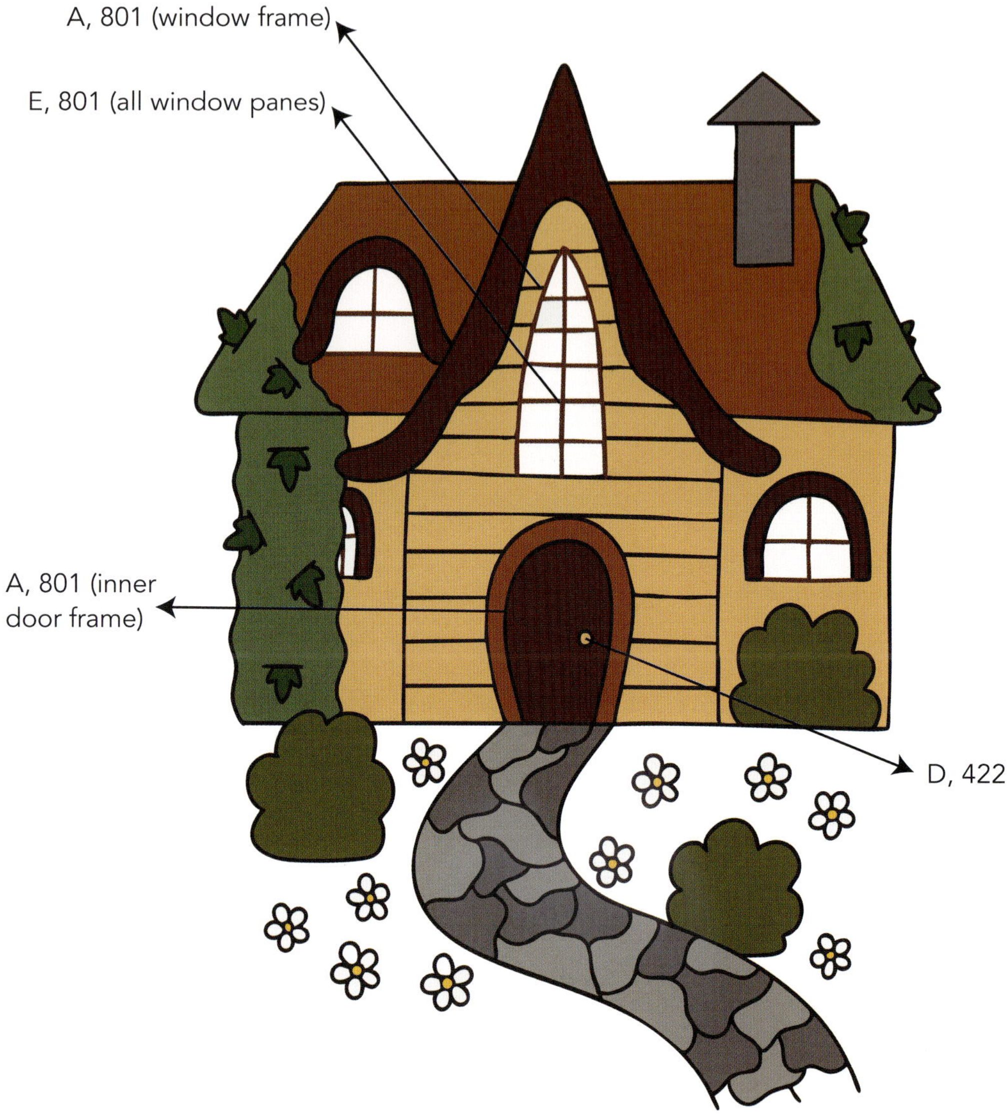

STITCH GUIDE

C	801	C	169	C	731	D	3822
C	869	C	317	C	3052	H	B5200
C	422	C	839	C	3051		

Cottage template, page 104

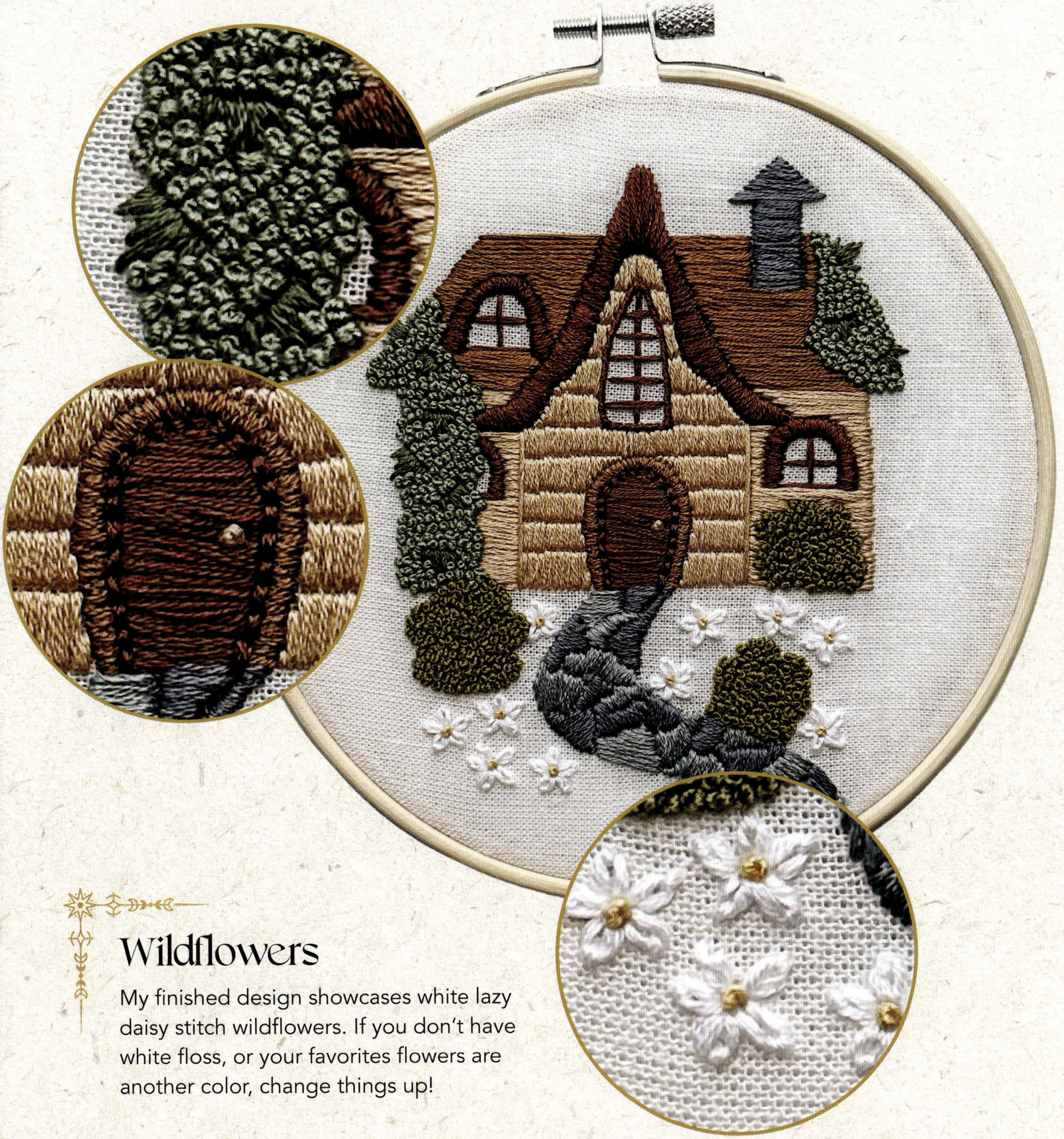

Wildflowers

My finished design showcases white lazy daisy stitch wildflowers. If you don't have white floss, or your favorites flowers are another color, change things up!

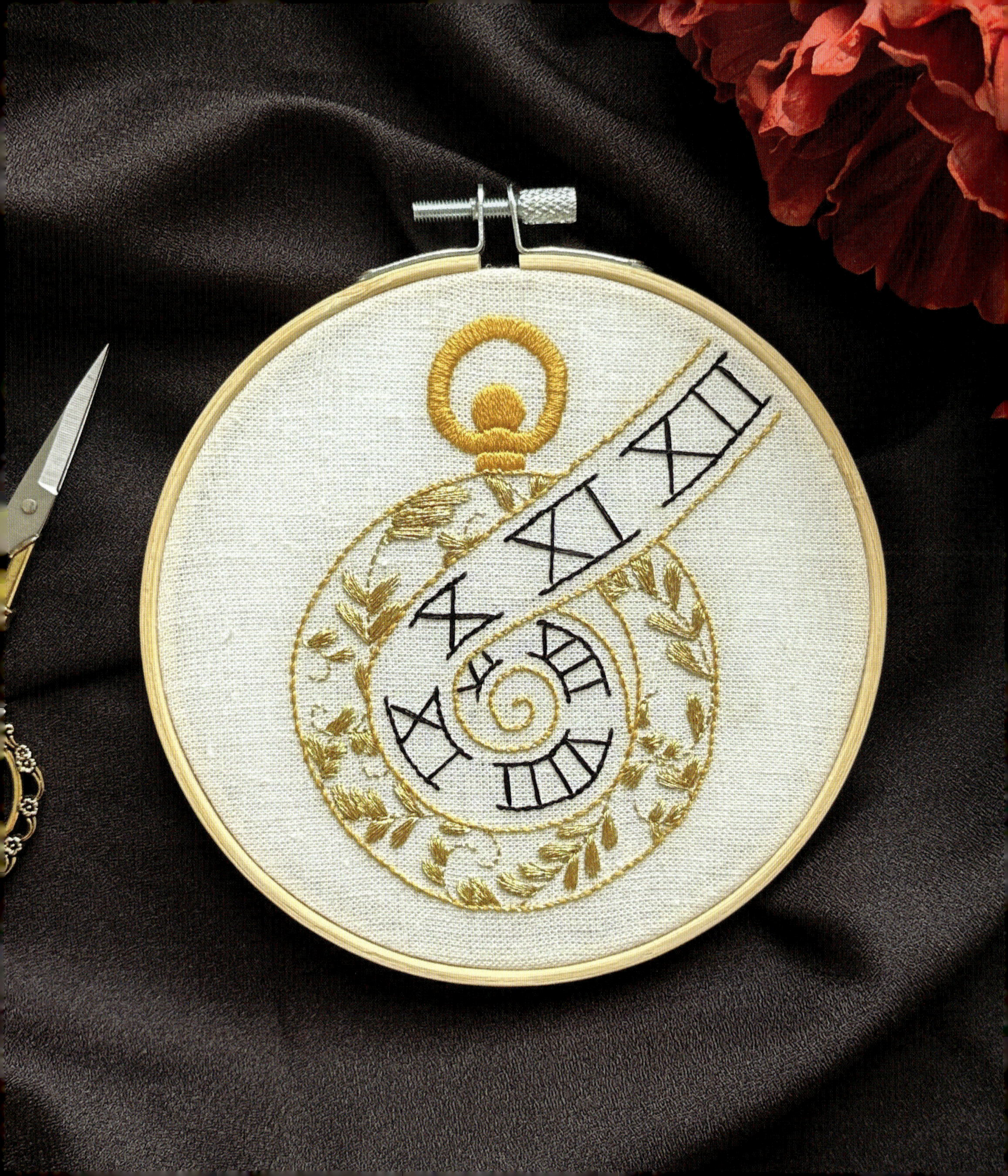

Time Travel Love

Tick … stitch … swoon. This pocket watch design celebrates romances that span centuries. Swirling clock hands, antique details, and soft metallic accents bring the magic of time travel to life. Perfect for dreamers, science nerds, and anyone who still believes fate has a schedule.

SUPPLIES

5" (13 cm) Embroidery Hoop

Fabric

Fabric Scissors

Embroidery Needle

Embroidery Scissors

STITCHES

Whipped Backstitch (A): page 11

Satin Stitch (C): page 12

Straight Stitch (E): page 13

THREADS

DMC Floss Colors

310

3820

D3821

Note

Use three strands of floss throughout, except for D3821, use one strand.

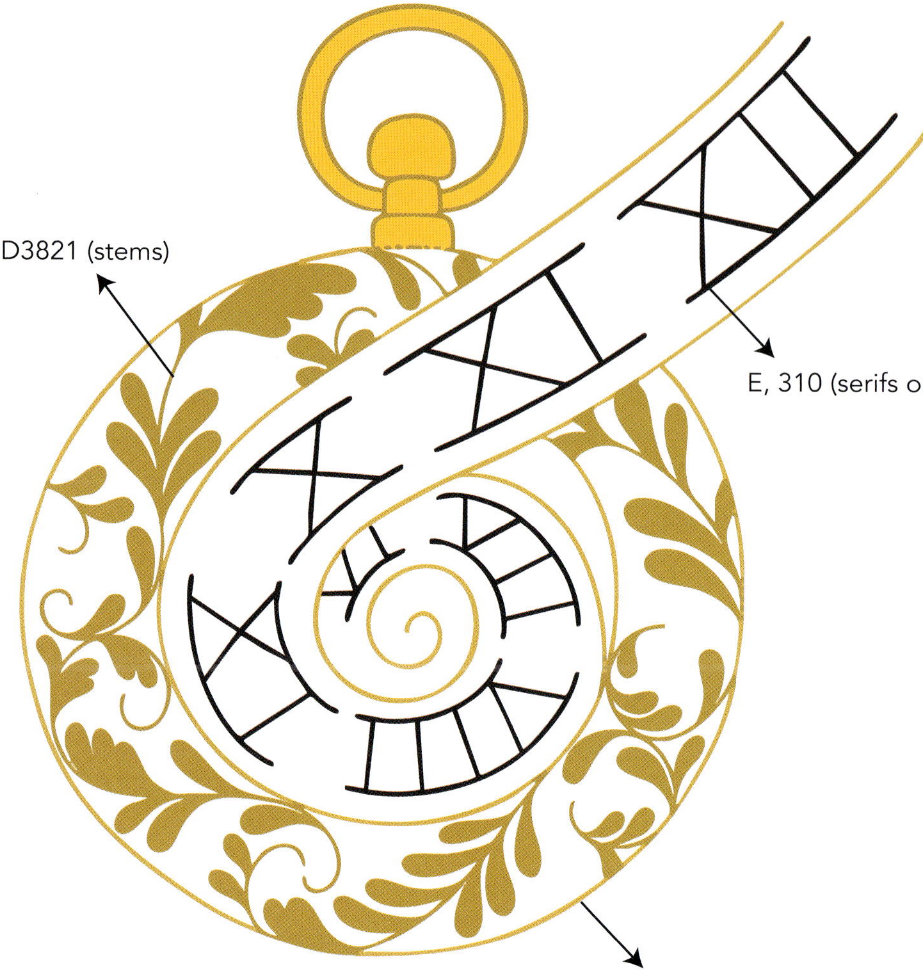

STITCH GUIDE

C	D3821
C	3820
A	310

Pocket Watch template, page 105

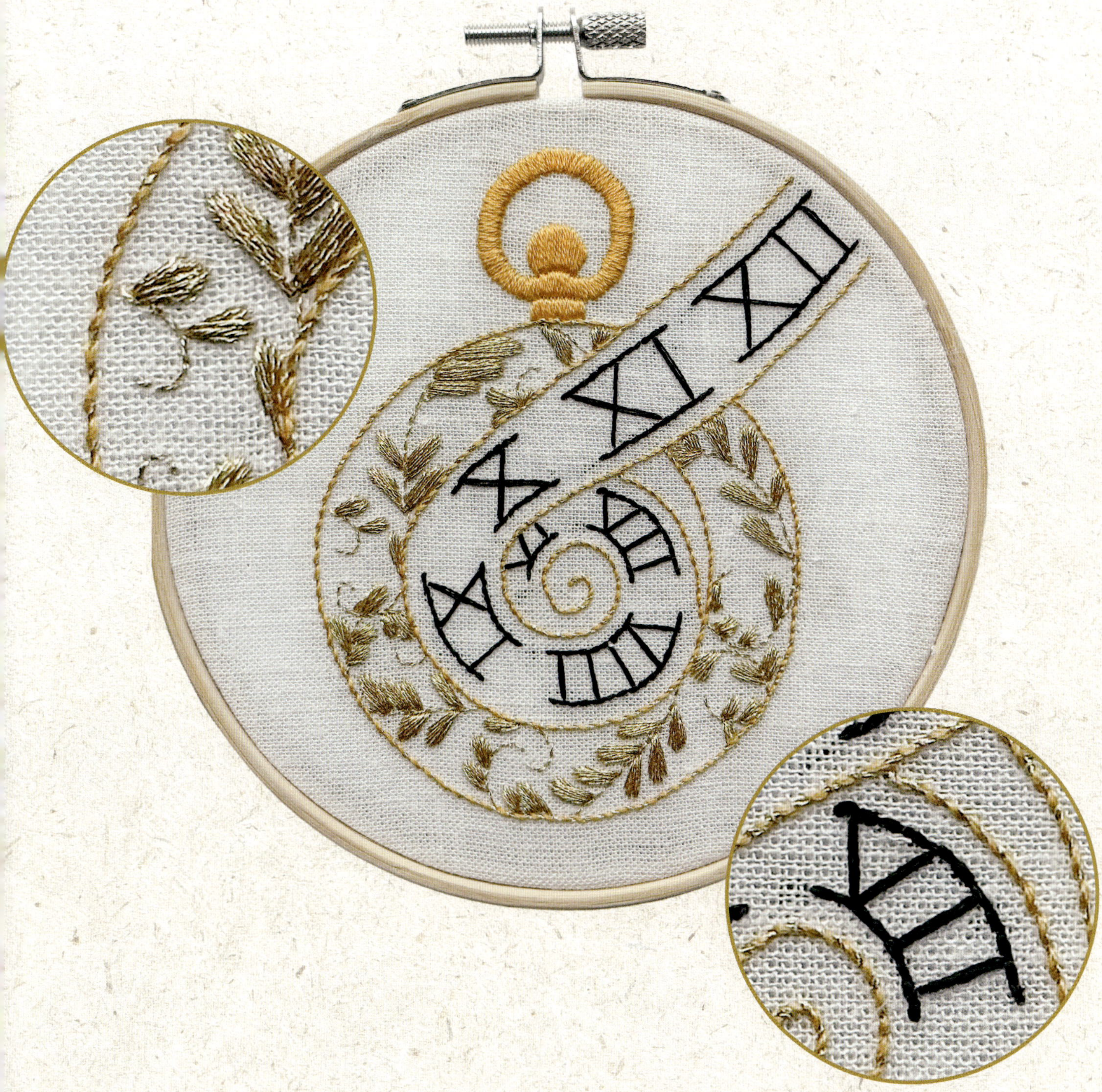

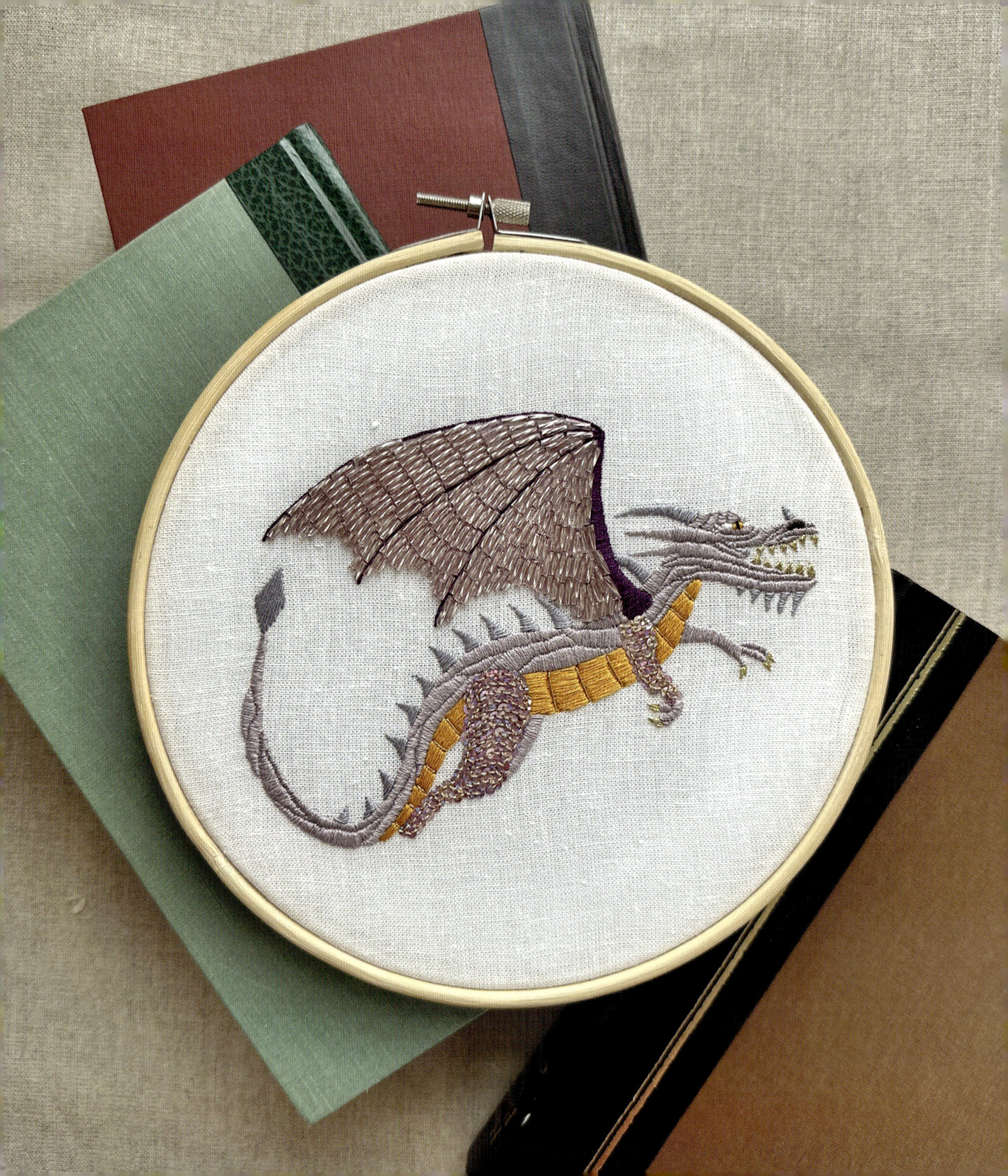

The Dragon

Not all dragons are meant to be slain. This majestic beast is decked out in sequins, beads, and dramatic flair. Equal parts protector and power symbol, it's a showstopping stitch with serious sparkle. Go bold, go extra! This dragon demands attention.

SUPPLIES

8" (20 cm) Embroidery Hoop

Fabric

Fabric Scissors

Embroidery Needle

Embroidery Scissors

Fine Beading Needle (or small embroidery needle)

6 mm Twisted Bugle Beads (light pink)

2 mm Sequins (pink)

STITCHES

Whipped Backstitch (A): page 11

Satin Stitch (C): page 12

Straight Stitch (E): page 13

THREADS

DMC Floss Colors

310

318

550

3042

3852

D3821

Note

Use three strands of floss throughout, except for D3821, use one strand.

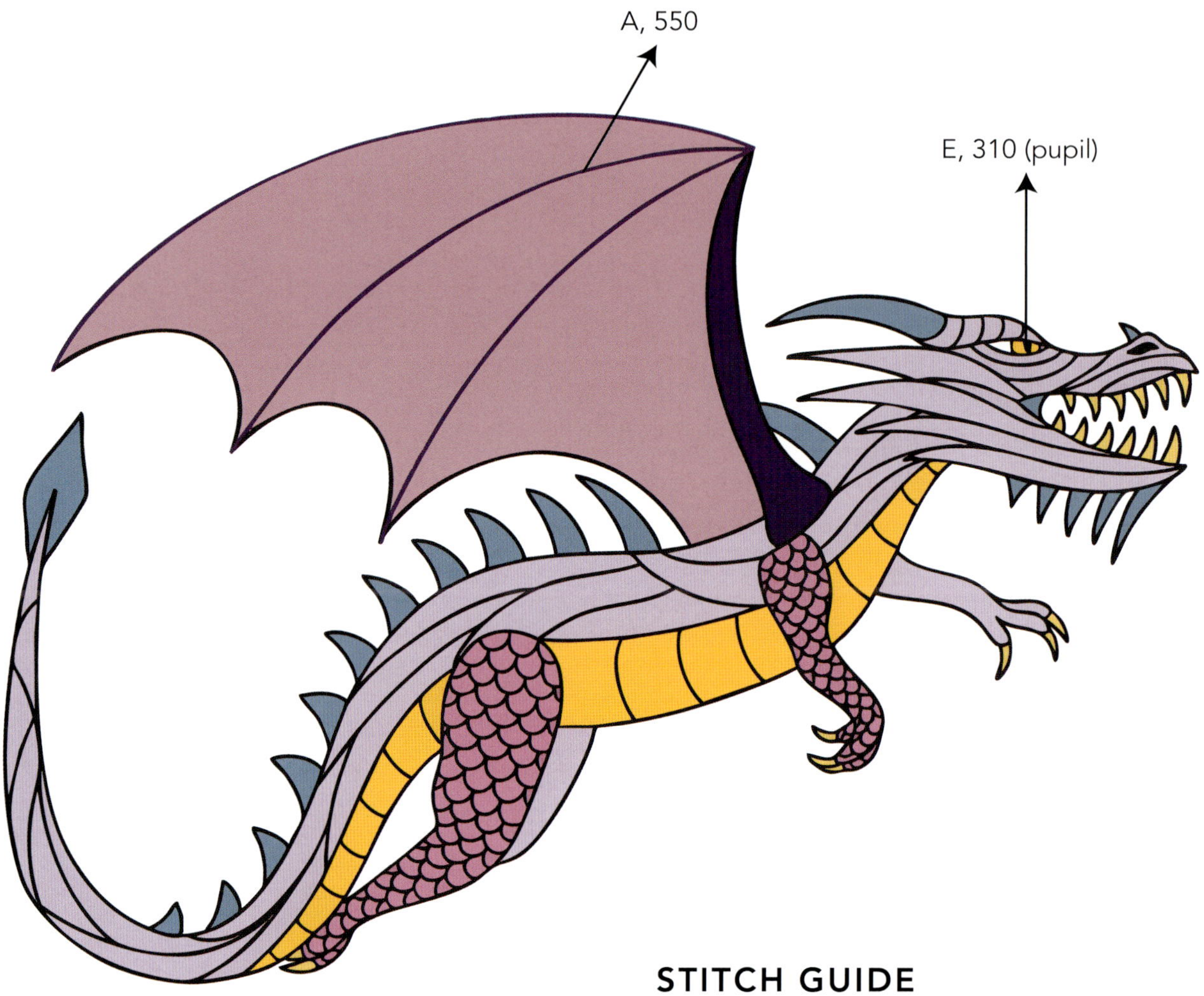

STITCH GUIDE

C 550	C 3042
Bugle Beads	C 3852
C 318	C D3821
Sequins	C 310

Dragon template, page 104

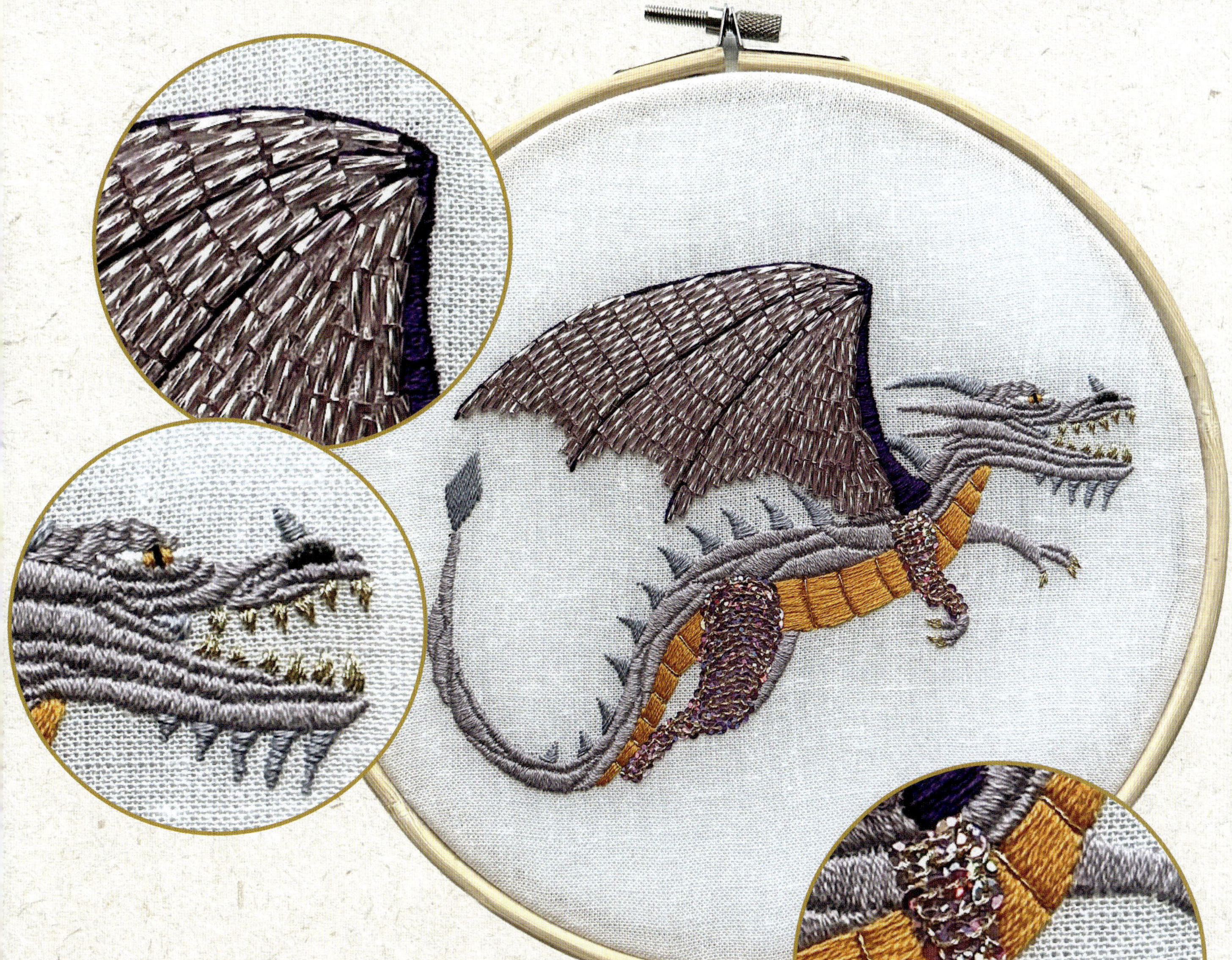

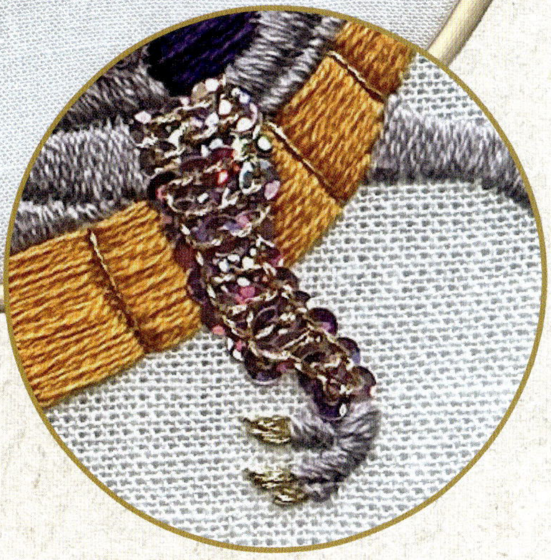

Beaded Embroidery

Bugle beads and flat sequins add sparkle and dimension to this spectacular dragon. If you're new to using beads in your embroidery, see page 16.

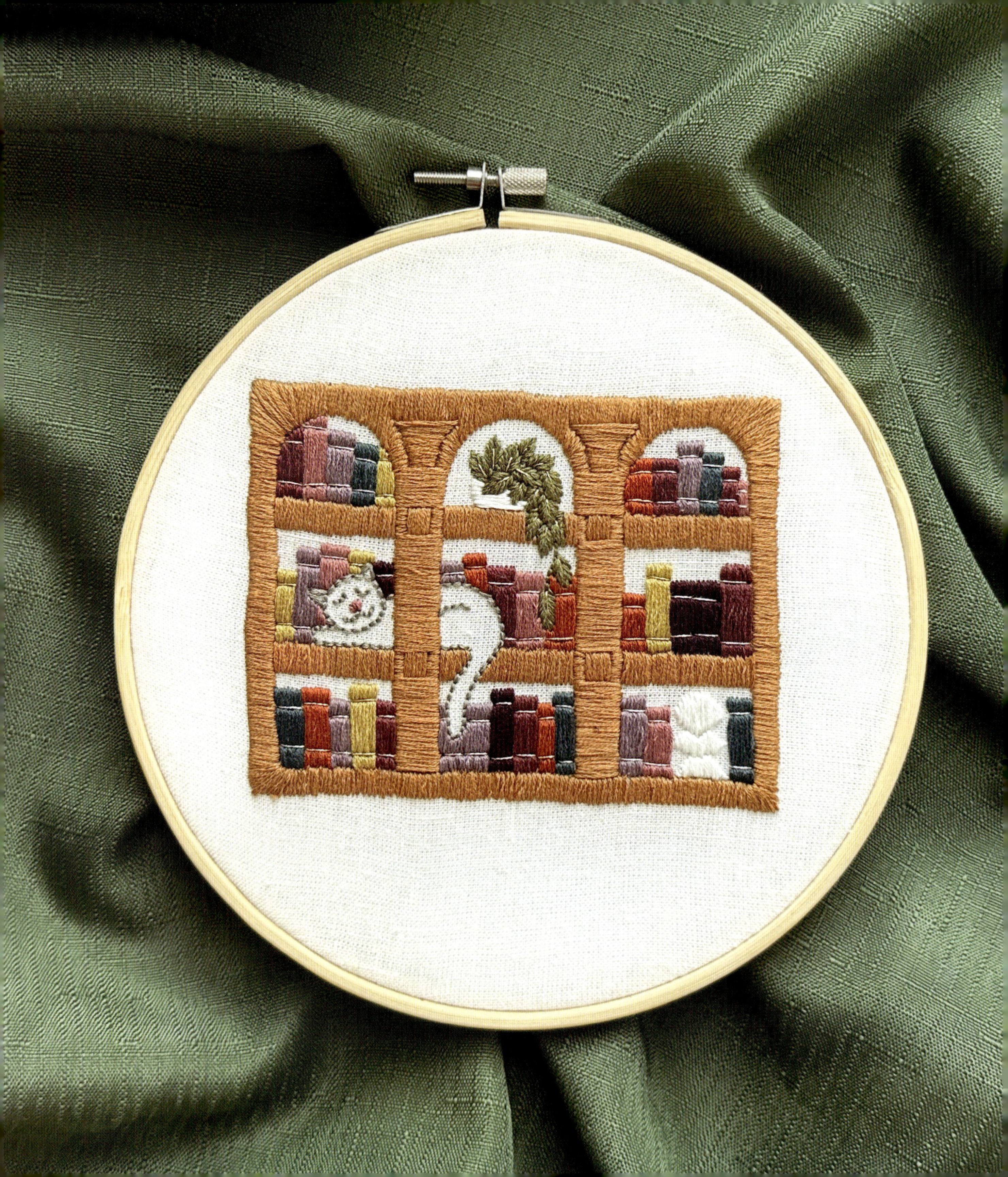

The Library Cat

Soft paw, loud purr, eternal guardian of the TBR. This cozy design features a curled-up cat snoozing on a library shelf because every magical reading space needs a feline familiar. Stitch it in soft neutrals or give your bookish kitty a fantasy twist.

SUPPLIES

7" (18 cm) Embroidery Hoop

Fabric

Fabric Scissors

Embroidery Needle

Embroidery Scissors

STITCHES

Backstitch (B): page 11

Satin Stitch (C): page 12

Straight Stitch (E): page 13

Fishbone Stitch (G): page 13

THREADS

DMC Floss Colors

154	3041
435	3726
646	3802
833	3865
918	D168 (optional)
924	D3821 (optional)
3011	

Note

Use six strands of floss throughout, except for D168 and D3821, use one strand.

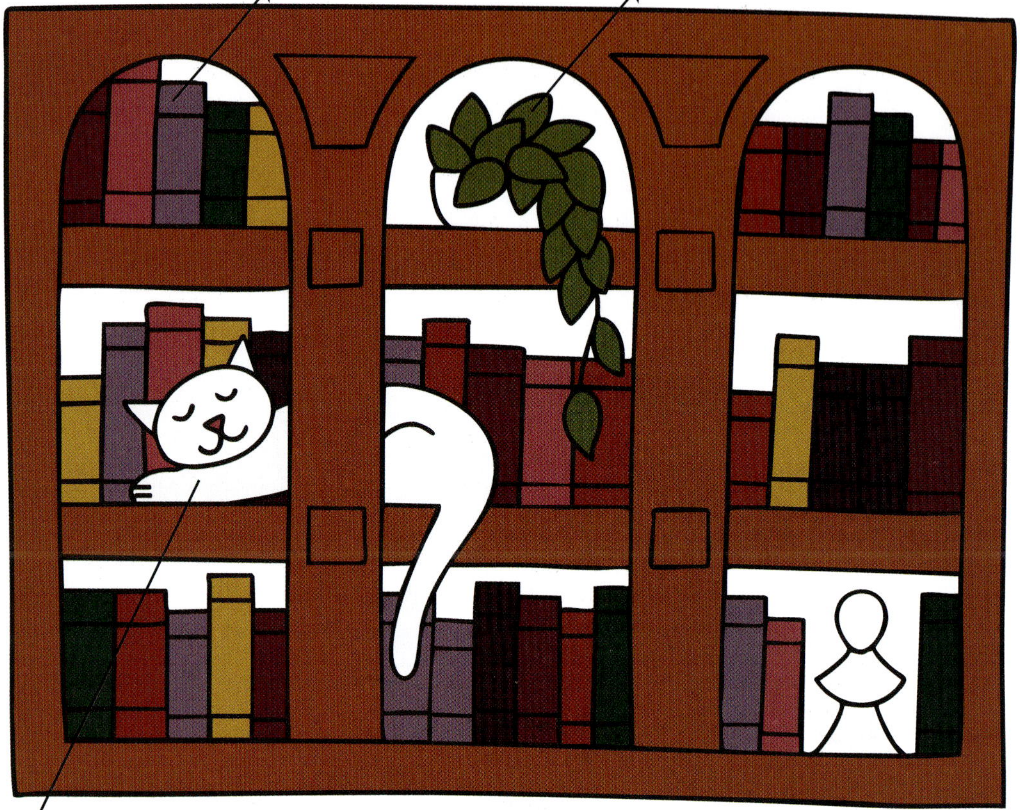

STITCH GUIDE

C 435	C 3041	C 833	C 3865
C 3802	C 3726	C 924	B 646, cat
C 154	G 3011	C 918	B 3011, vines

Optional

C D3821   C D168

Library Shelves template, page 106

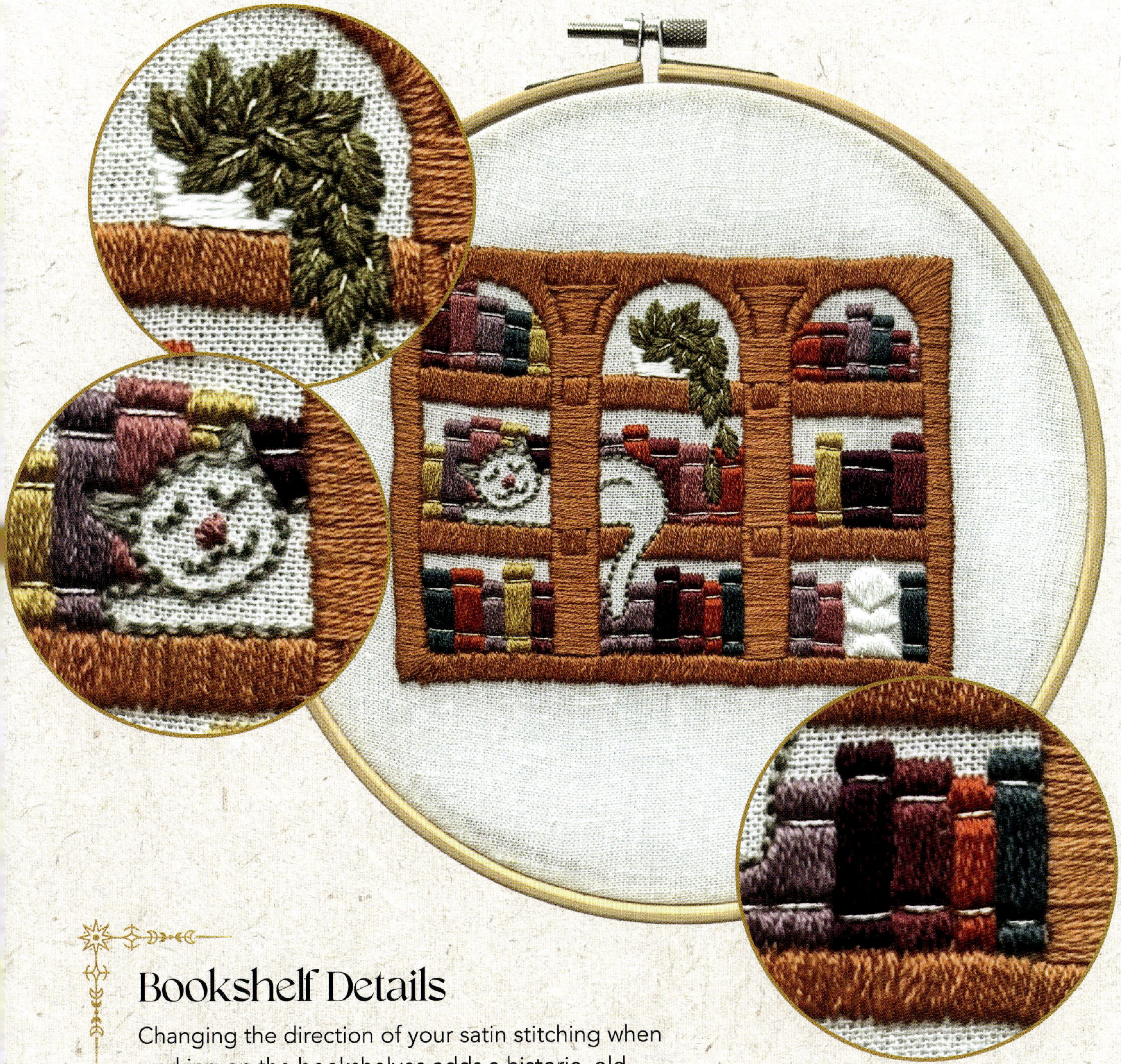

Bookshelf Details

Changing the direction of your satin stitching when working on the bookshelves adds a historic, old-world touch reminiscent of decorative moldings and mortise and tenon joinery.

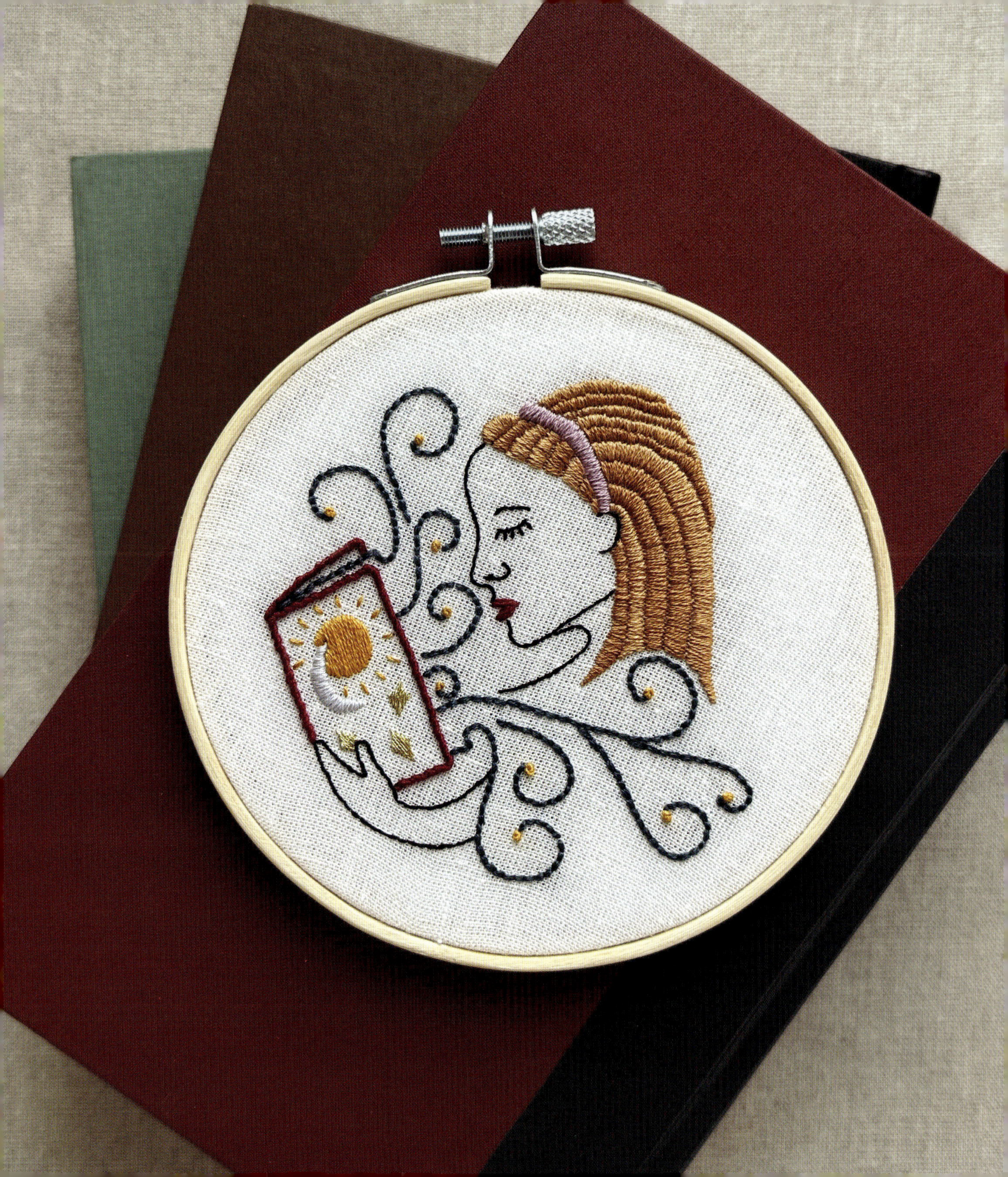

Ink Drinker

For the readers who devour stories like oxygen. "Ink Drinker" is a French phrase with bite and beauty, stitched here with dramatic scrollwork details. Display it in your reading nook or add it to a tote bag so everyone knows you came prepared to read *and* slay.

SUPPLIES

5" (13 cm) Embroidery Hoop

Fabric

Fabric Scissors

Embroidery Needle

Embroidery Scissors

STITCHES

Backstitch (B): page 11

Satin Stitch (C): page 12

French Knots (D): page 12

Straight Stitch (E): page 13

THREADS

DMC Floss Colors

310	3685
435	3747
436	3836
930	3852
	D3821

Note

Use six strands of floss throughout, except for the areas outlined in black; use three strands in these areas. Use one strand for D3821.

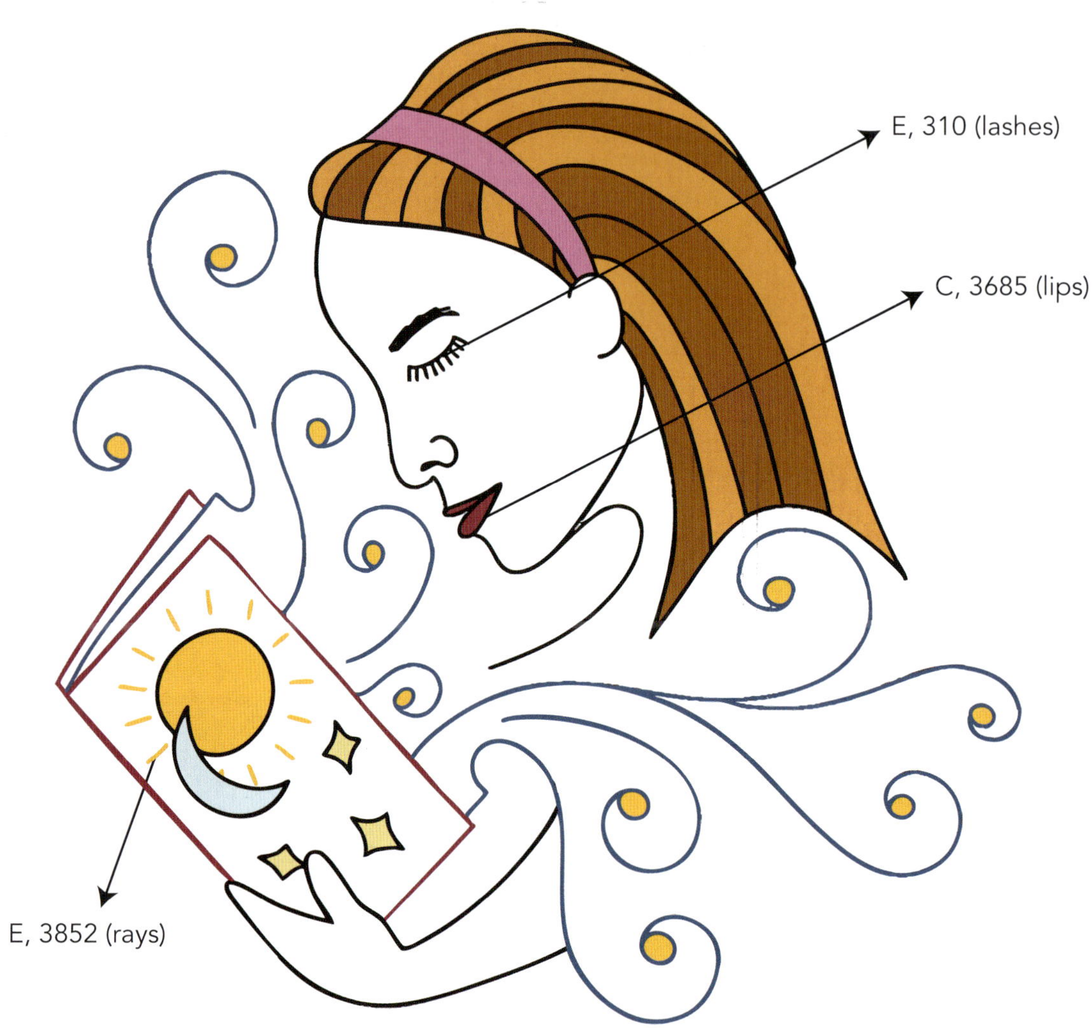

STITCH GUIDE

C	3836	C	435	C	D3821
B	930	A	3685	A	310
C	436	D	3852	C	3747

Ink Drinker template, page 107

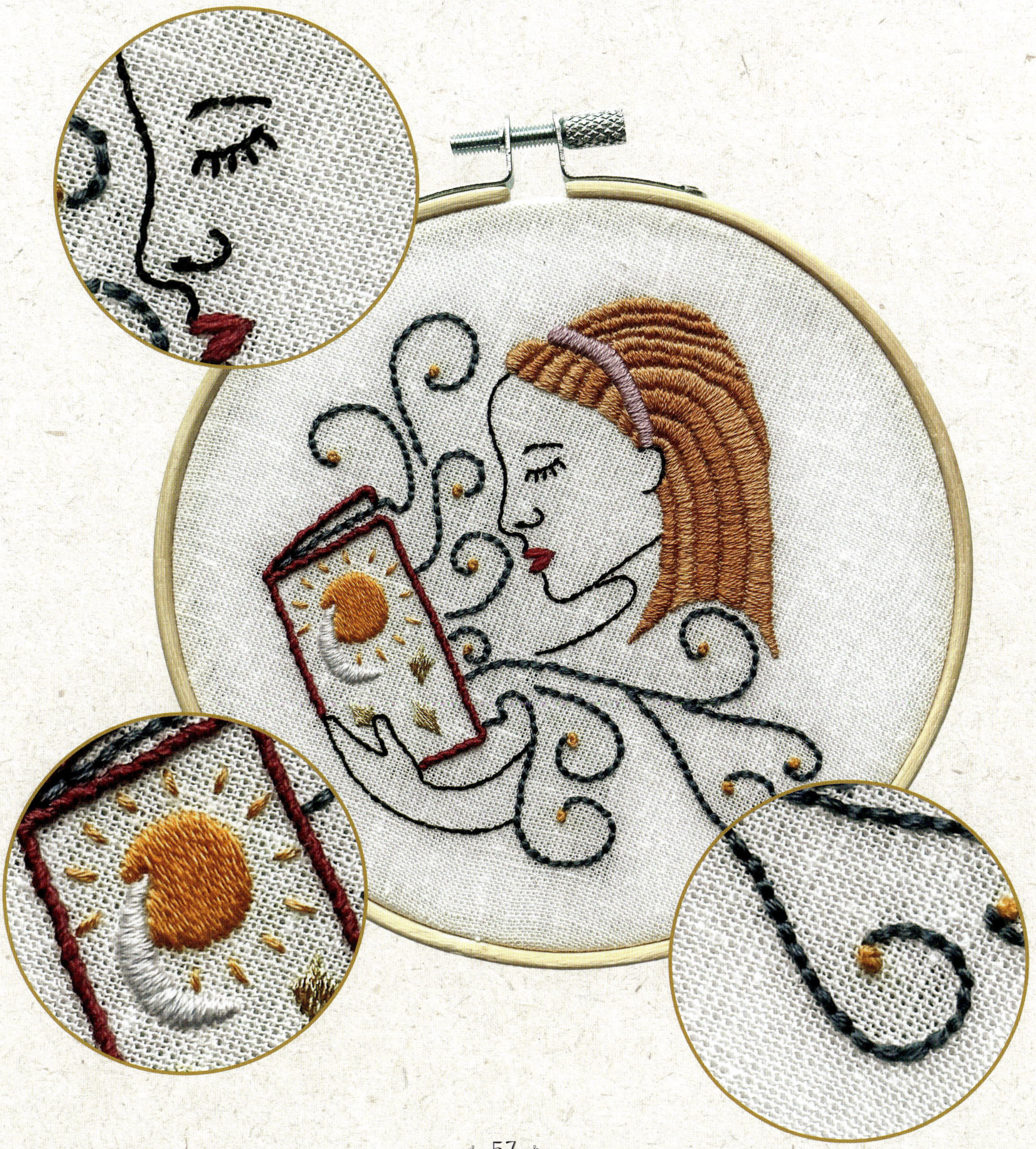

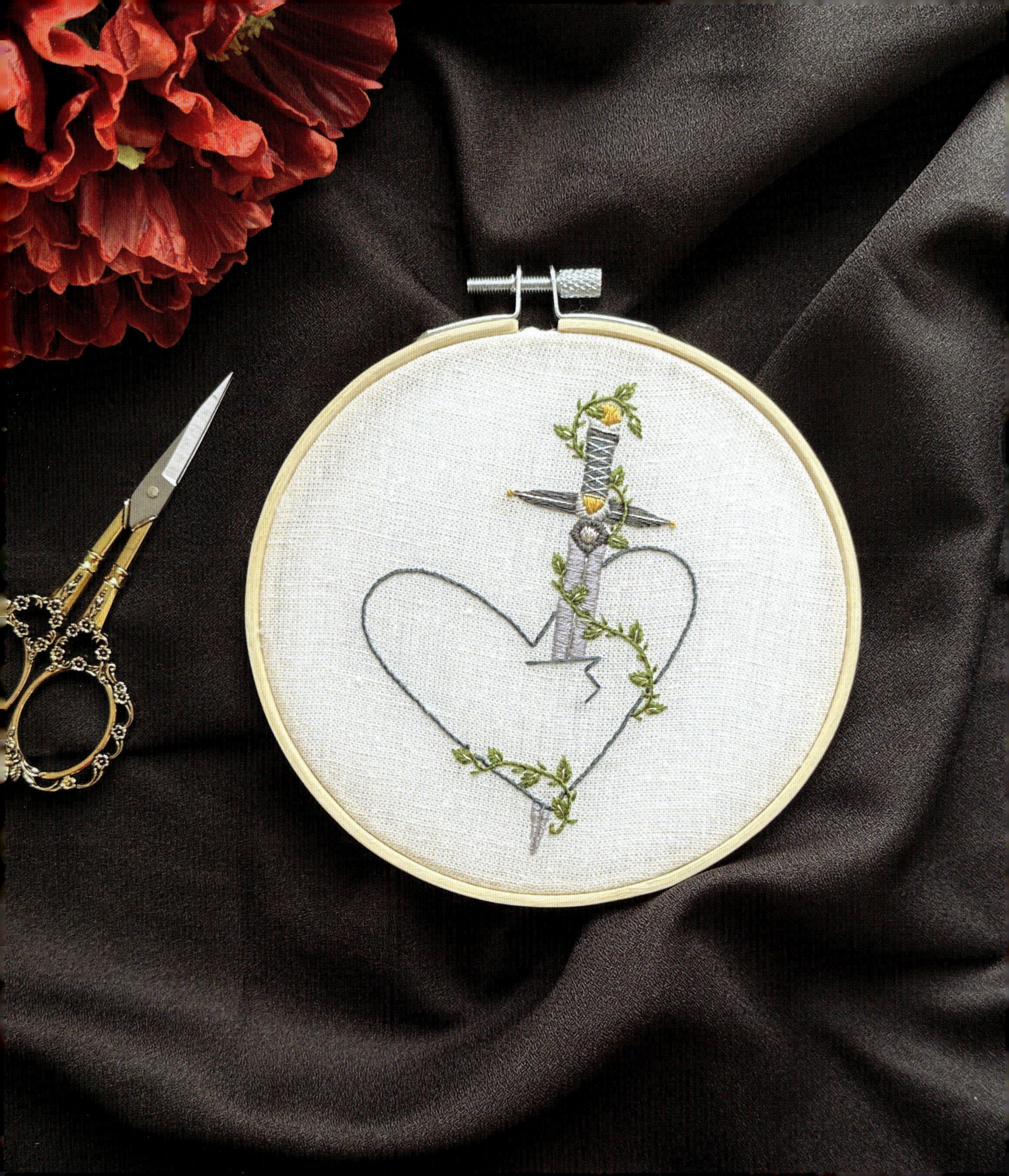

Enemies to Lovers

Sharp words. Sharper tension. This design features a dagger plunged into a heart—because love sometimes hurts before it heals. A tribute to everyone's favorite trope, this piece practically begs for icy silvers and a little personal flair. Enemies to lovers? Always a yes.

SUPPLIES

5" (13 cm) Embroidery Hoop

Fabric

Fabric Scissors

Embroidery Needle

Embroidery Scissors

STITCHES

Whipped Backstitch (A): page 11

Satin Stitch (C): page 12

French Knots (D): page 12

Straight Stitch (E): page 13

Fishbone Stitch (G): page 13

THREADS

DMC Floss Colors

318

469

930

3799

3820

D168

Note

Use three strands of floss throughout, except for D168, use one strand.

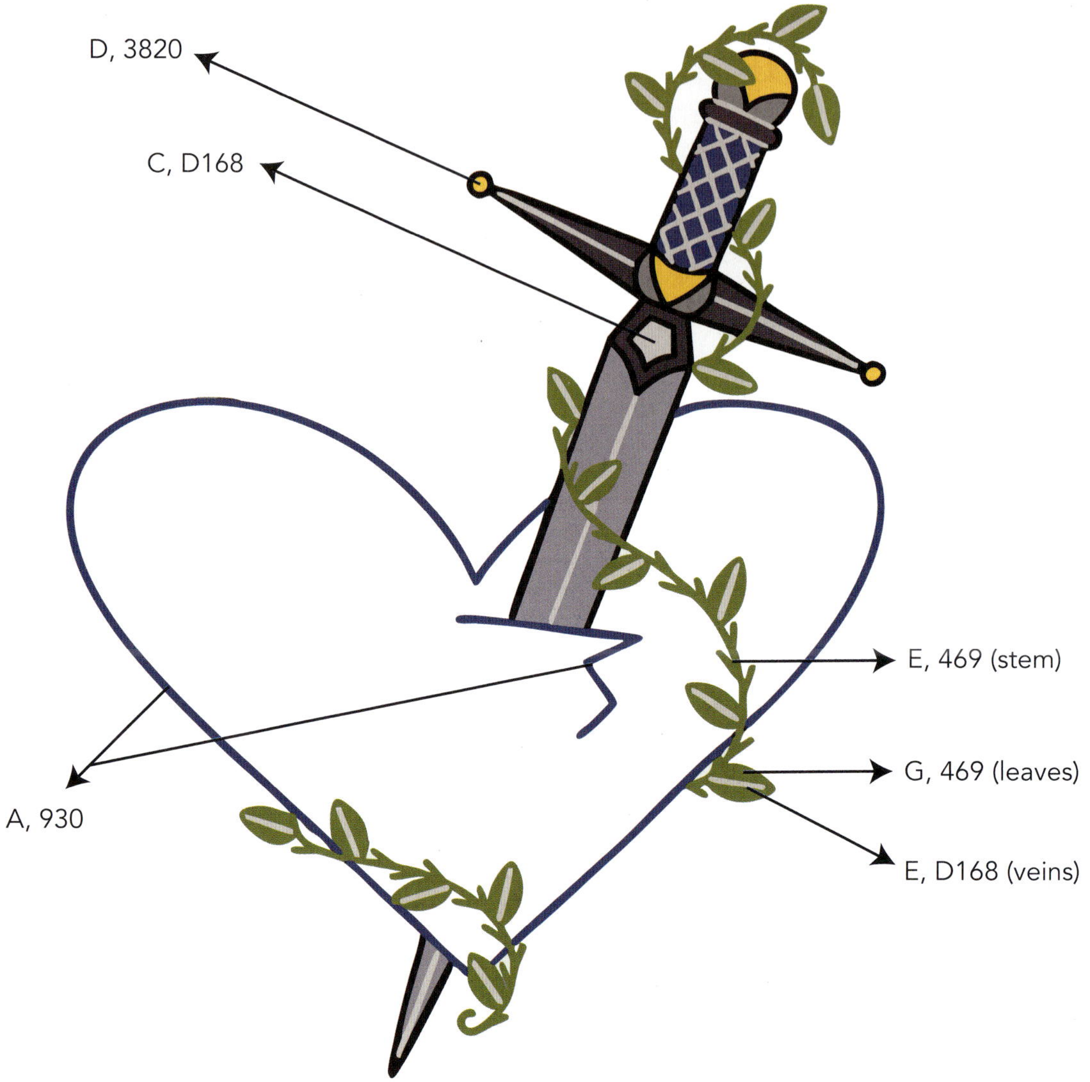

Heart and Sword template, page 107

STITCH GUIDE

C	930	C	318
A	469	E	D168
C	3799	C	3820

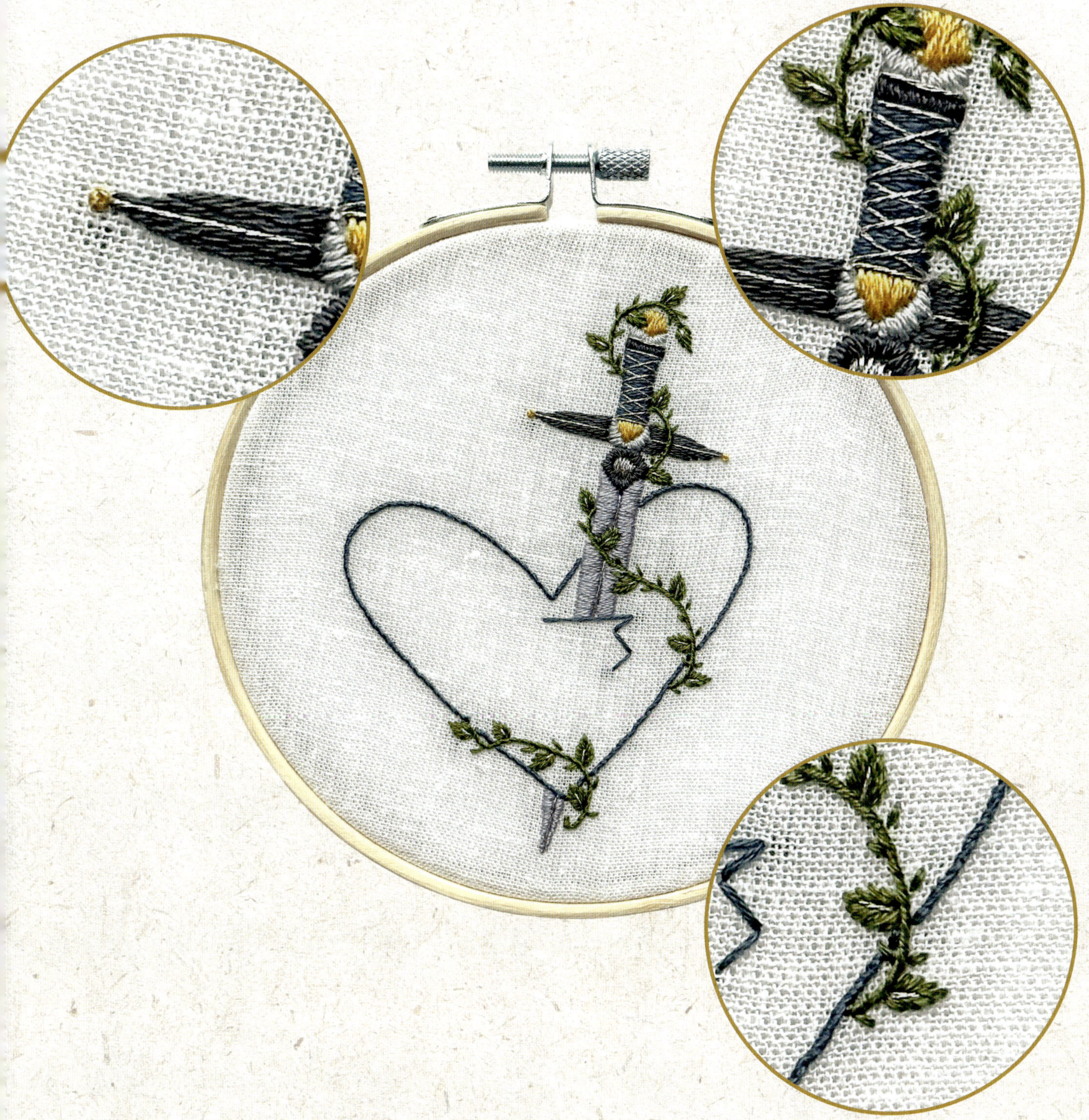

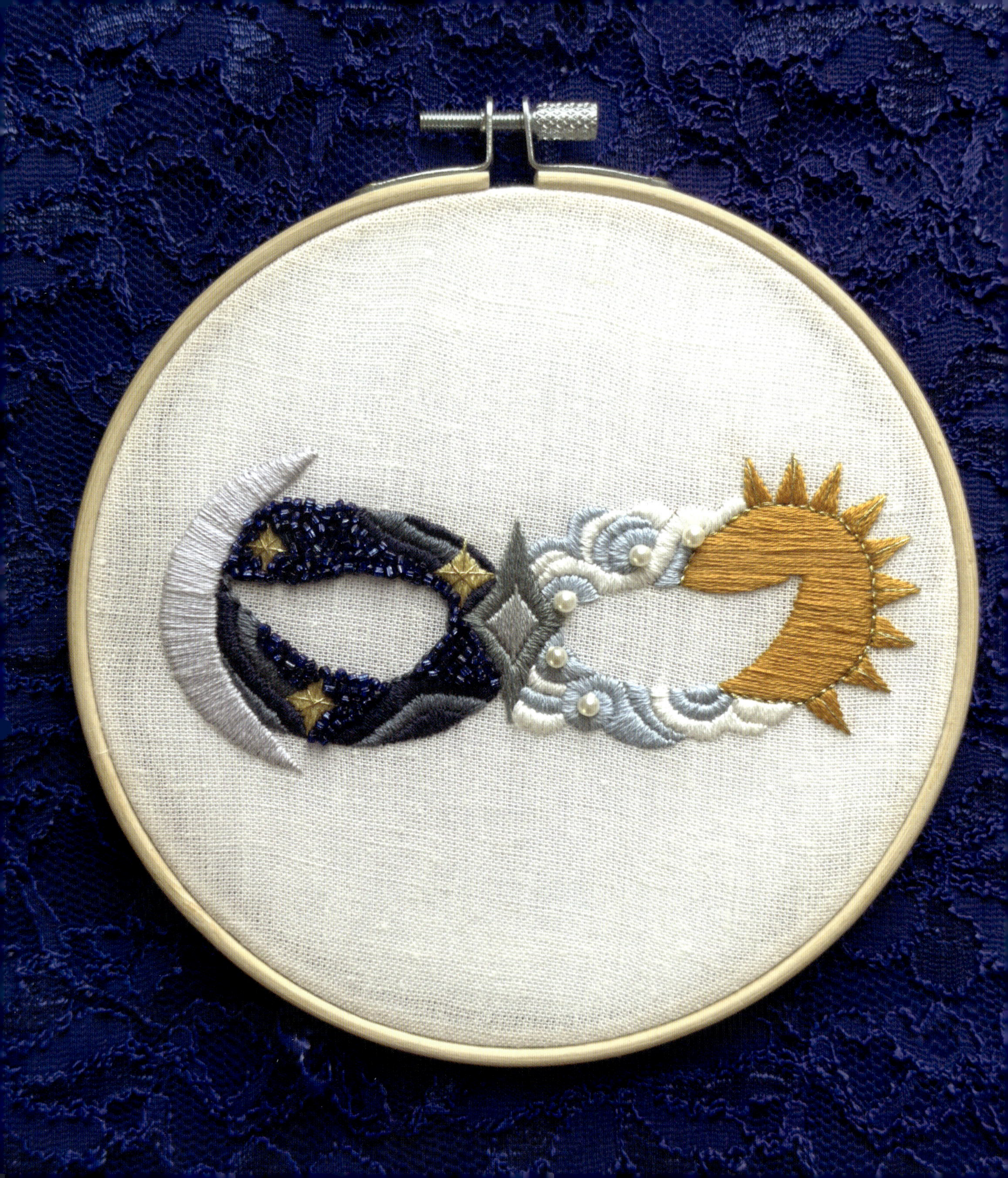

Masquerade Mystery

Hidden identities, forbidden glances, and that one unforgettable night. This embroidered mask shimmers with secret intentions and glittering beadwork. Whether stitched in classic black or jewel-toned drama, it's a nod to every romantasy moment where nothing is quite what it seems … and the stakes are deliciously high.

SUPPLIES

6" (15 cm) Embroidery Hoop

Fabric

Fabric Scissors

Embroidery Needle

Embroidery Scissors

Fine Beading Needle (or small embroidery needle)

2 mm Seed Beads (dark blue)

3 mm Faux Pearl Beads

STITCHES

Backstitch (B): page 11

Satin Stitch (C): page 12

Straight Stitch (E): page 13

THREADS

DMC Floss Colors

168	3747
336	3822
800	3852
926	3865
931	D3821

Note

Use three strands of floss throughout, except for D3821, use one strand.

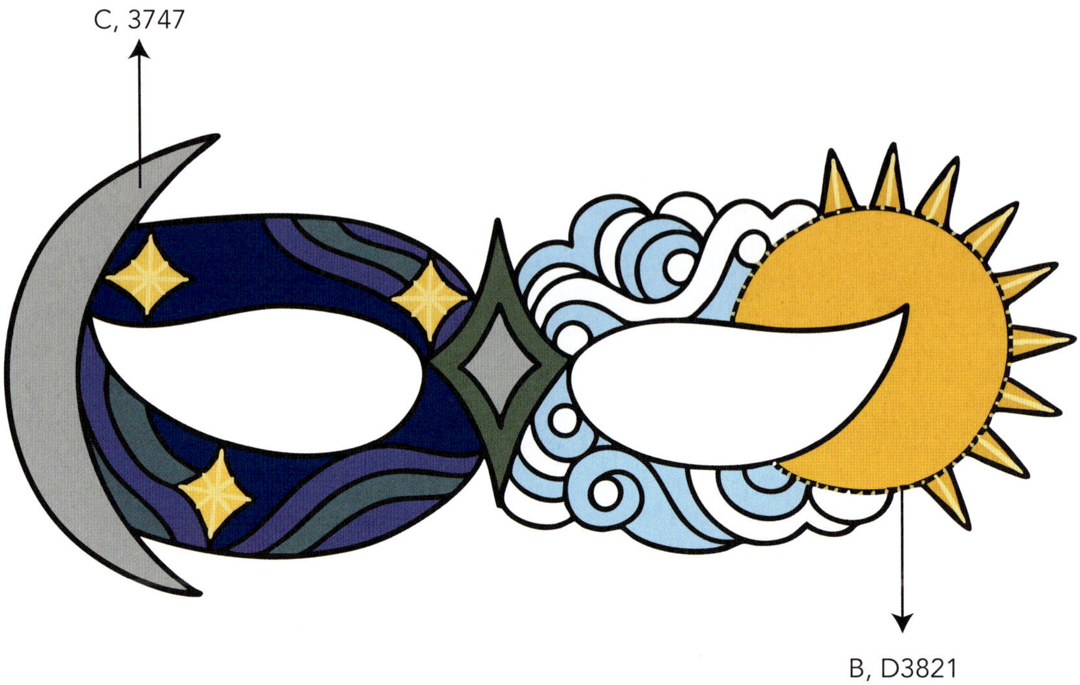

STITCH GUIDE

Stitch	Color	Stitch	Color	Stitch	Color	Stitch	Color
C	336	C	168	C	3822	C	3865
C	931	E	D3821	C	800		
C	926	G	3852		Dark Blue Beads		

Mask template, page 105

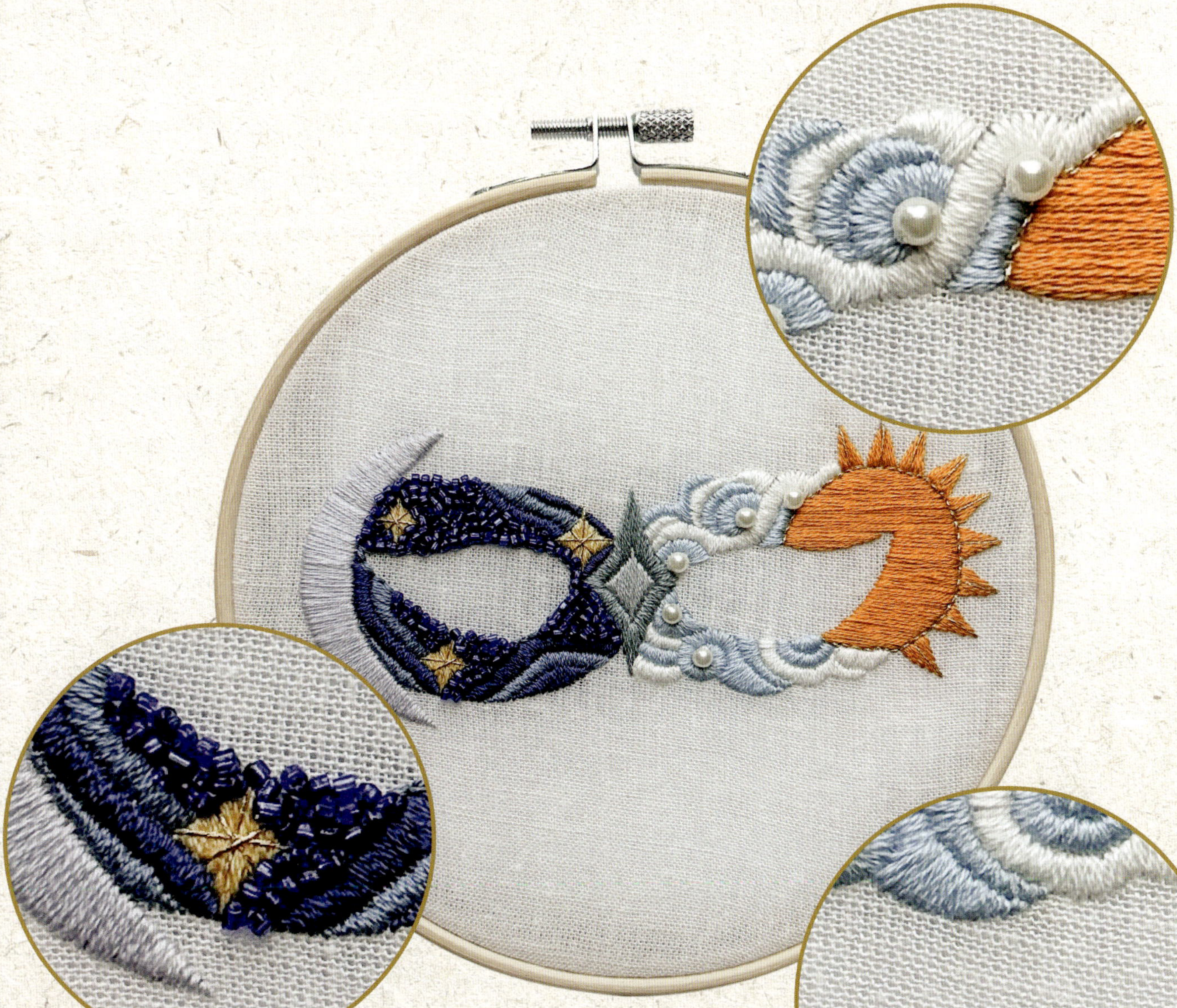

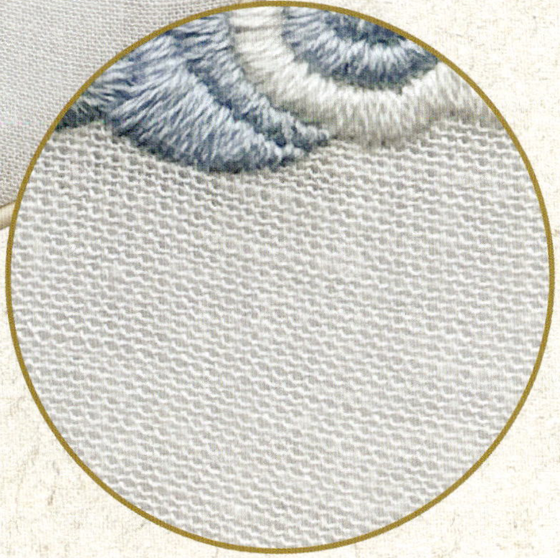

Beaded Embroidery

The seed beads and pearls that embellish this mask add to the glitz and glamour of a night full of mystery. If you're new to using beads in your embroidery, see page 16.

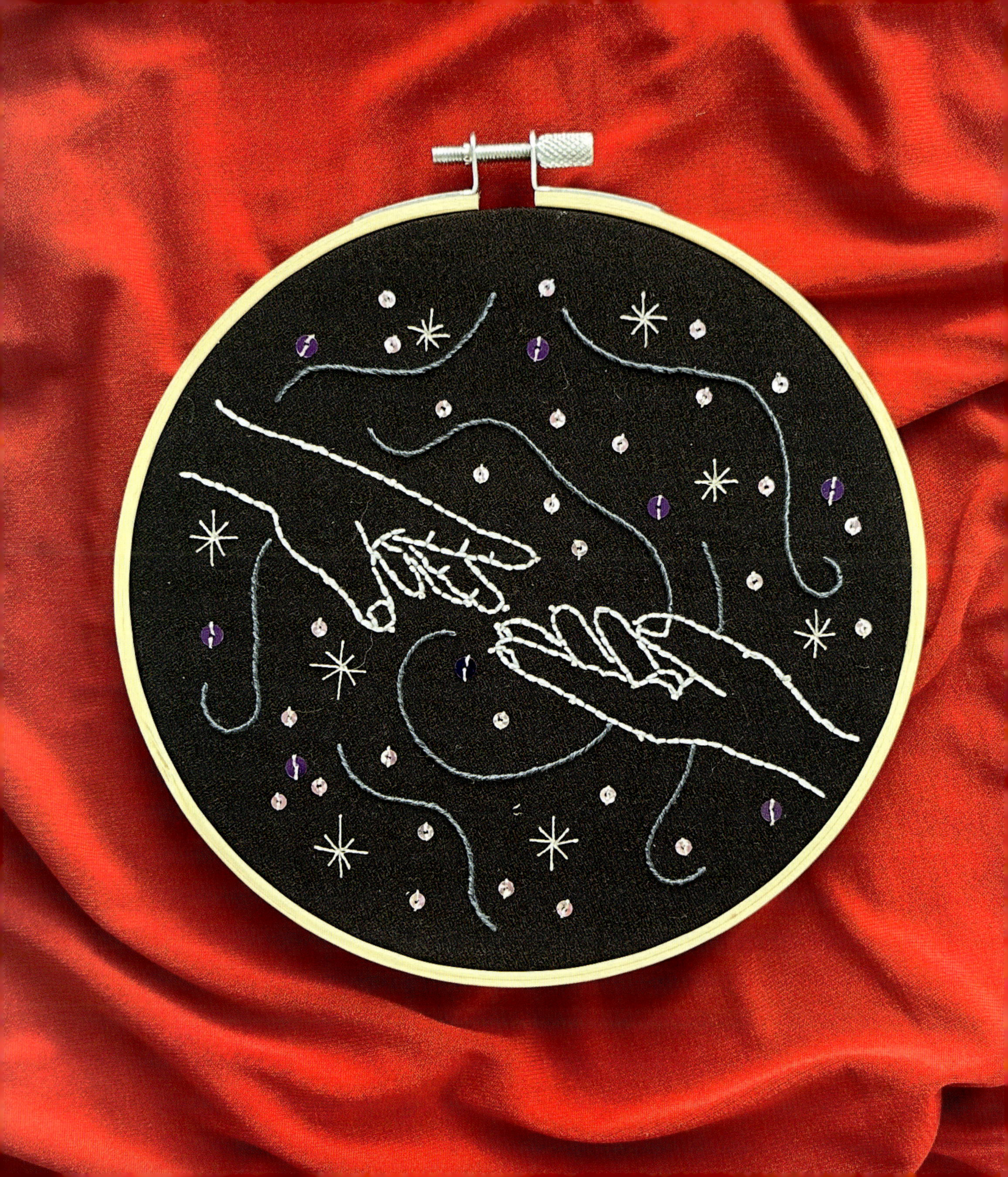

Star-Crossed Romance

A love written in the stars and doomed all the same. This constellation-inspired pattern traces two hands reaching for each other, yet just out of touch. Add tiny stitched stars or a trail of shimmer. Heart-wrenching? Maybe. Beautiful? Absolutely.

SUPPLIES

6" (15 cm) Embroidery Hoop

Fabric

Fabric Scissors

Embroidery Needle

Embroidery Scissors

Sequins in two sizes (purple and silver)

STITCHES

Whipped Backstitch (A): page 11

Backstitch (B): page 11

French Knots (D): page 12

Straight Stitch (E): page 13

THREADS

DMC Floss Colors

168

930

D168

Note

Use three strands of floss throughout, except for D168, use one strand.

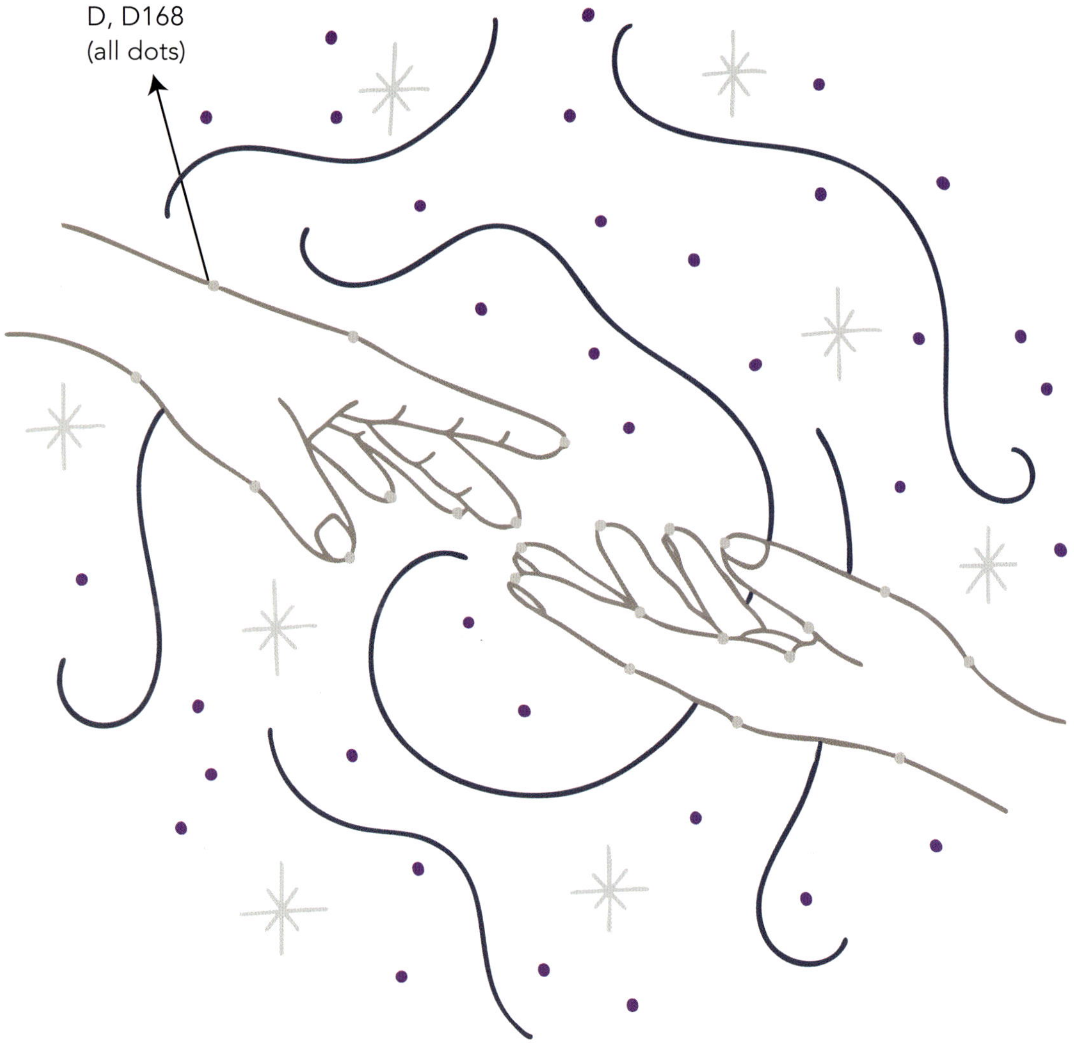

STITCH GUIDE

Night Sky template, page 108

A 930 B 168 E D168 Purple and silver sequins

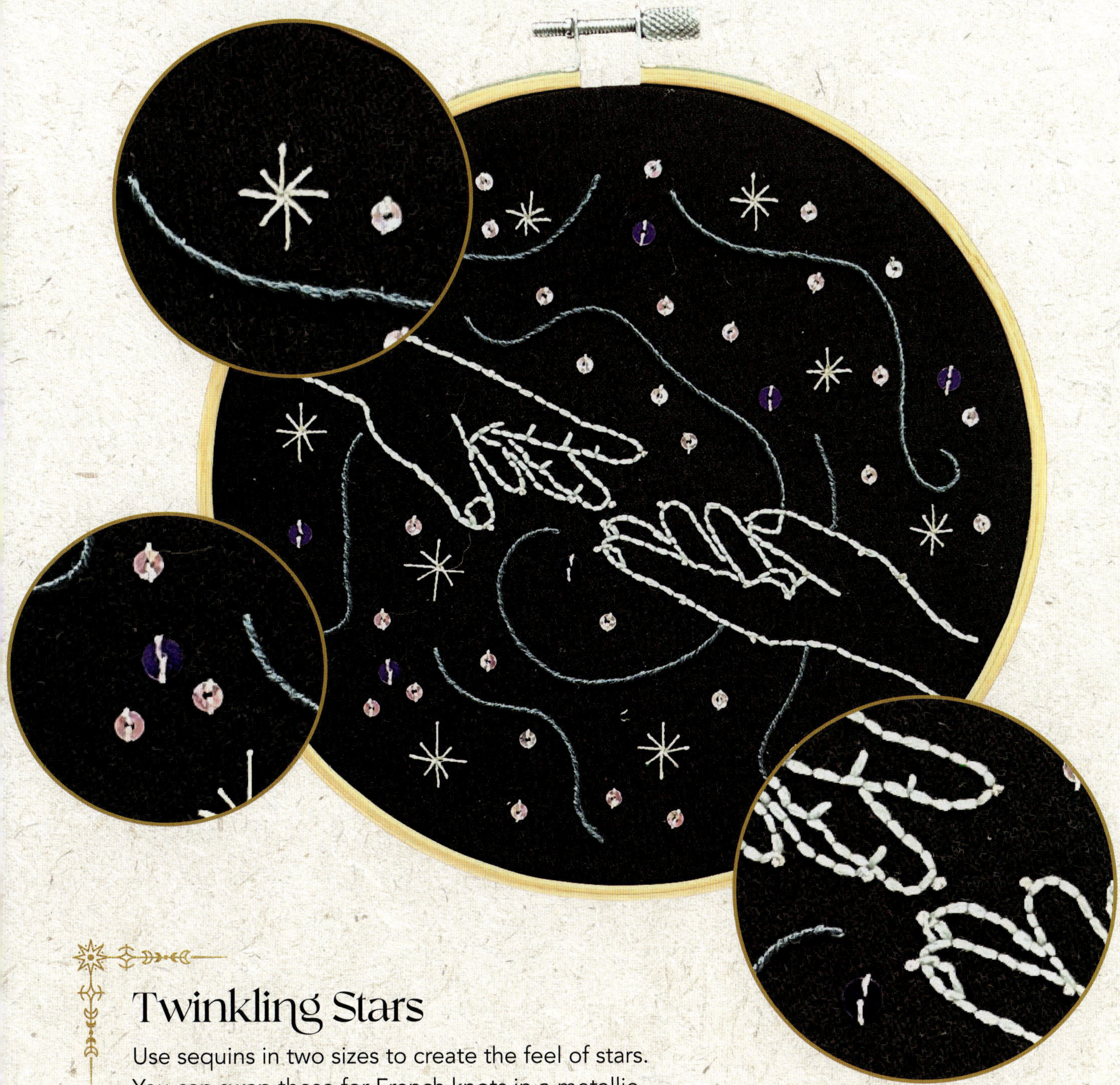

Twinkling Stars

Use sequins in two sizes to create the feel of stars. You can swap these for French knots in a metallic thread if you don't have sequins.

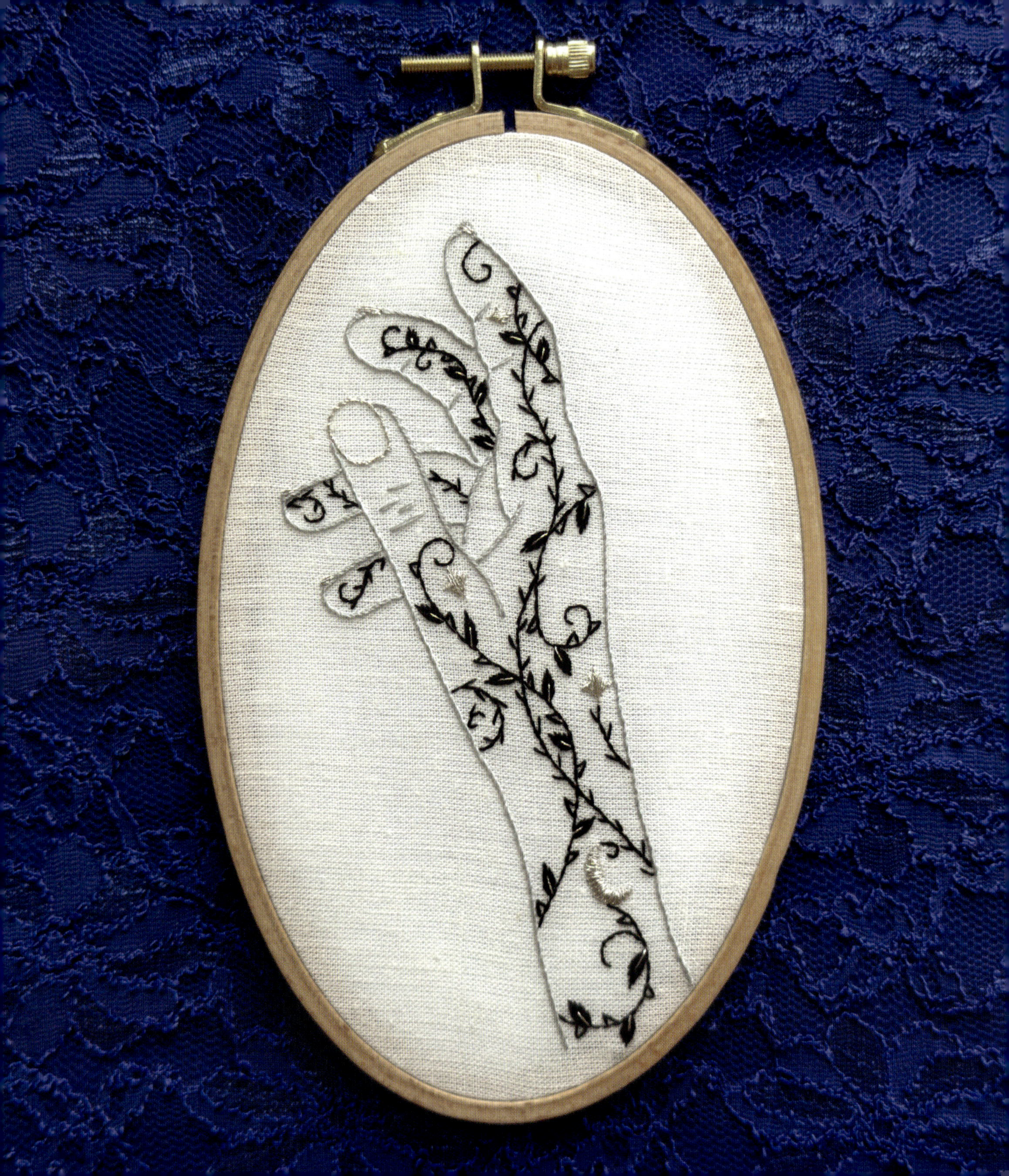

The Fae Bargain

Magic always comes at a cost. This design centers on a tattooed hand wrapped in twisting vines. It's a visual ode to the bargains that bind us, for better or worse. Ideal for variegated threads, metallic ink details, or a bit of moody embellishment. Sign carefully.

SUPPLIES

8 × 5" (20 × 13 cm) Oval Embroidery Hoop

Fabric

Fabric Scissors

Embroidery Needle

Embroidery Scissors

STITCHES

Whipped Backstitch (A): page 11

Satin Stitch (C): page 12

Straight Stitch (E): page 13

Fishbone Stitch (G): page 13

THREADS

DMC Floss Colors

168

310

D168

Note

Use three strands of floss throughout, except for D168, use one strand.

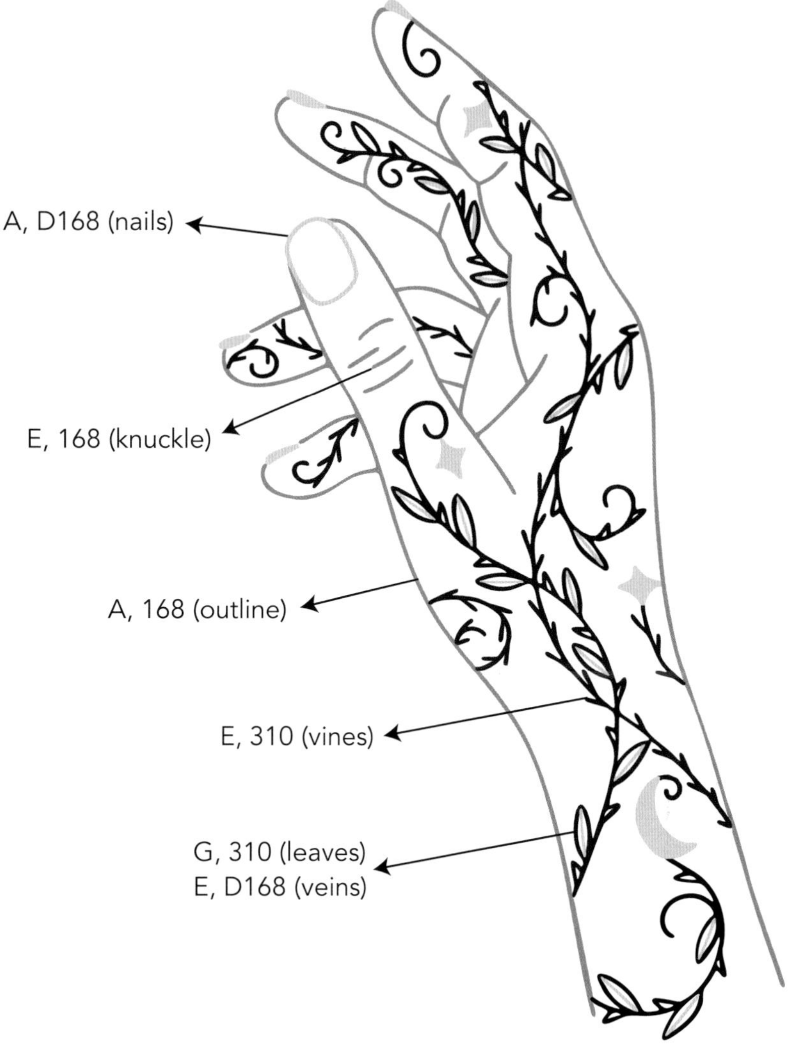

STITCH GUIDE

- A 168
- C D168
- A 310

Hand template, page 104

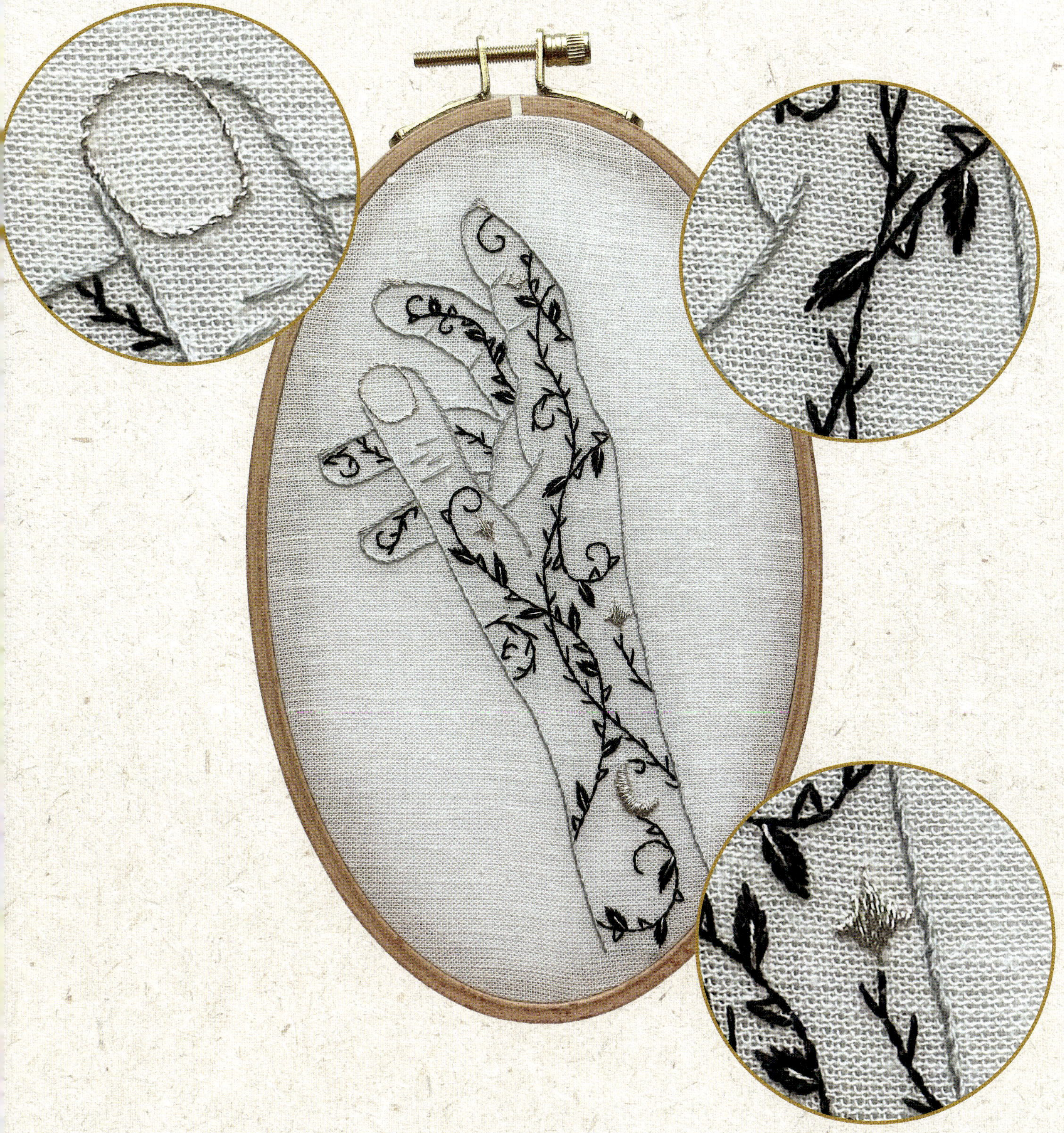

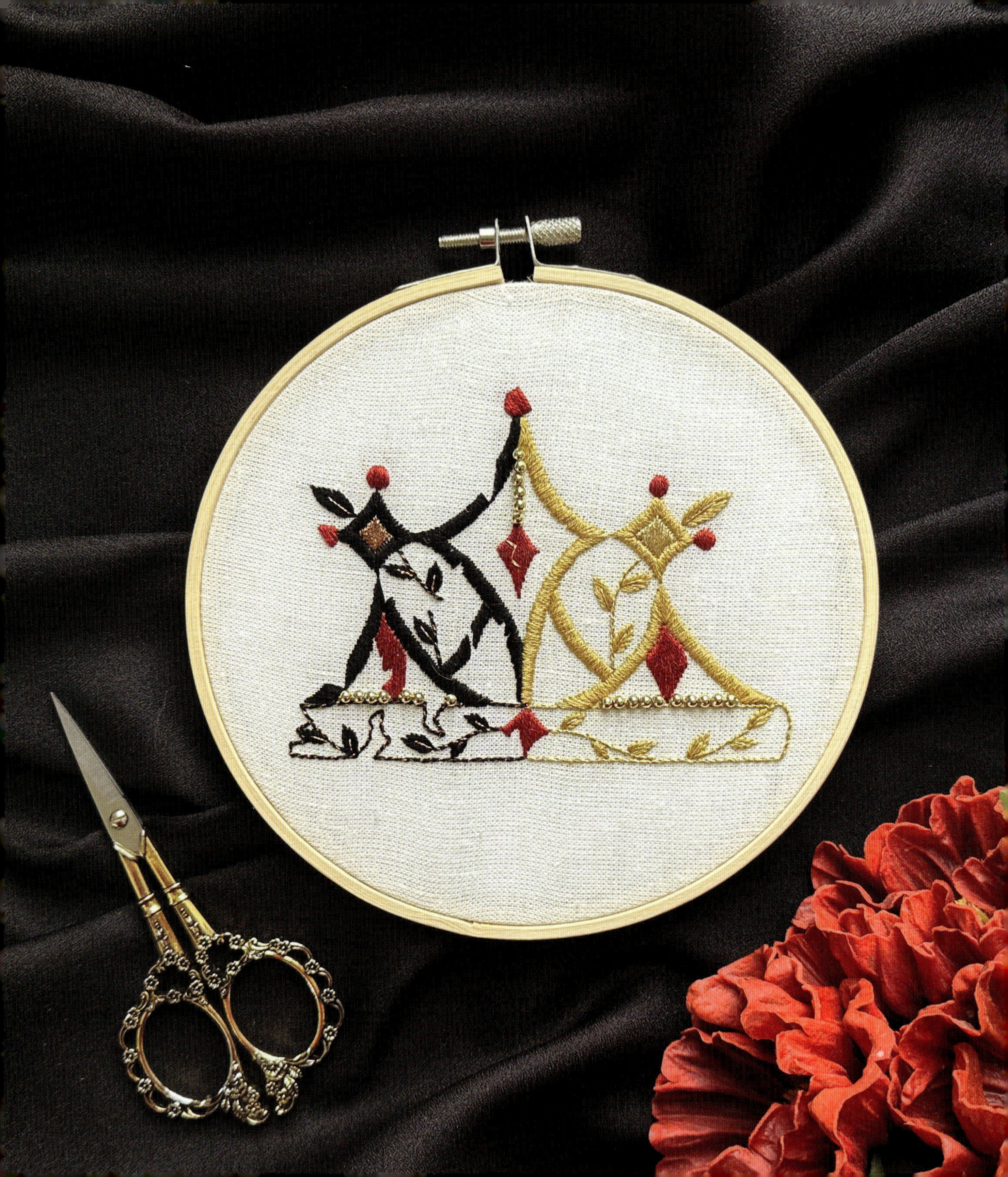

Shadow Crown

Redemption arcs hit hardest when the fall was spectacular. This half-shadowed crown symbolizes the villains who choose to change and the power that comes with that choice. Stitch it in high contrast: light and dark, gold and black, hope and heartbreak. It's never too late to be good-*ish*.

SUPPLIES

6" (15 cm) Embroidery Hoop

Fabric

Fabric Scissors

Embroidery Needle

Embroidery Scissors

2 mm Round Gold Beads

STITCHES

Whipped Backstitch (A): page 11

Satin Stitch (C): page 12

French Knots (D): page 12

Straight Stitch (E): page 13

Fishbone Stitch (G): page 13

THREADS

DMC Floss Colors

310

815

833

D301

D3821

Note

Use three strands of floss throughout, except for D301 and D3821, use one strand.

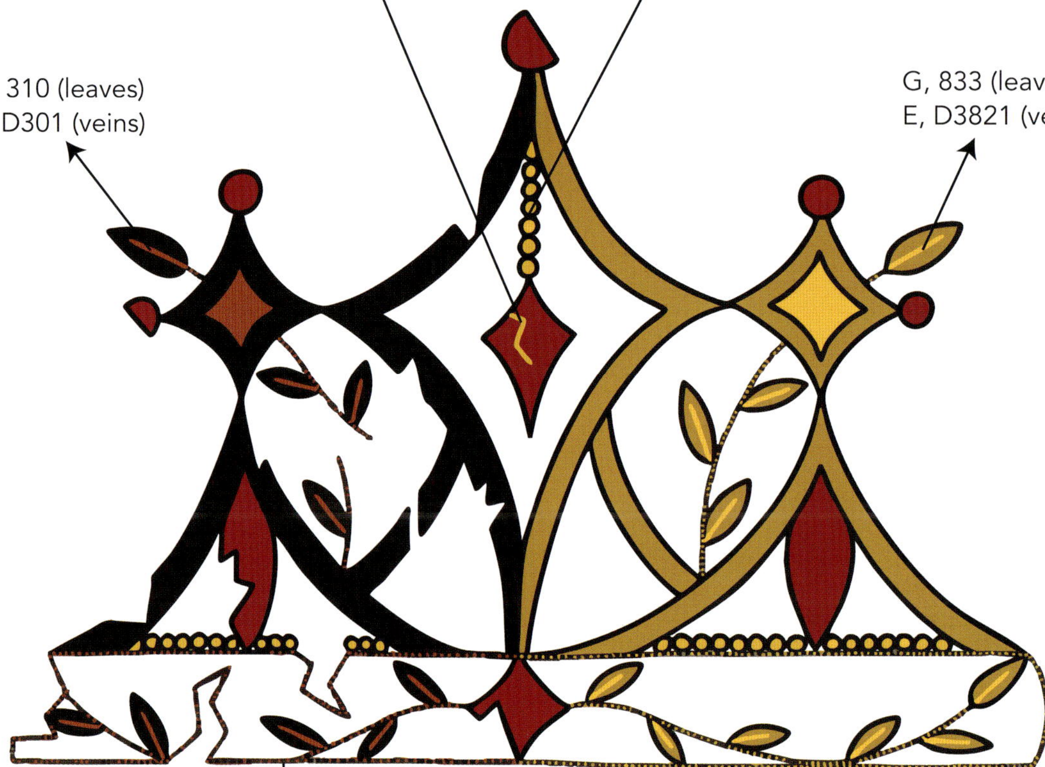

STITCH GUIDE

815
D301
833
D3821
310

Crown template, page 107

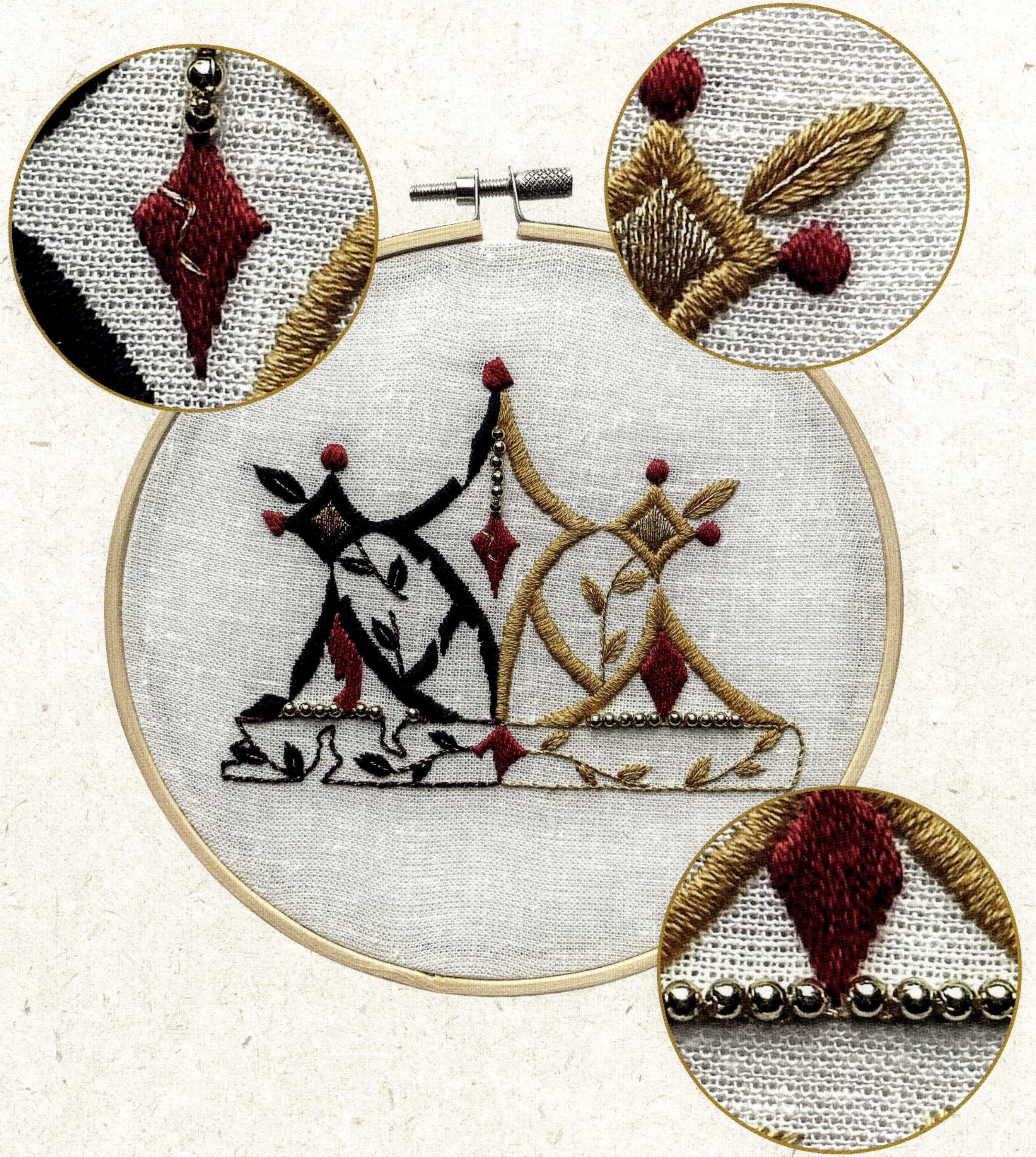

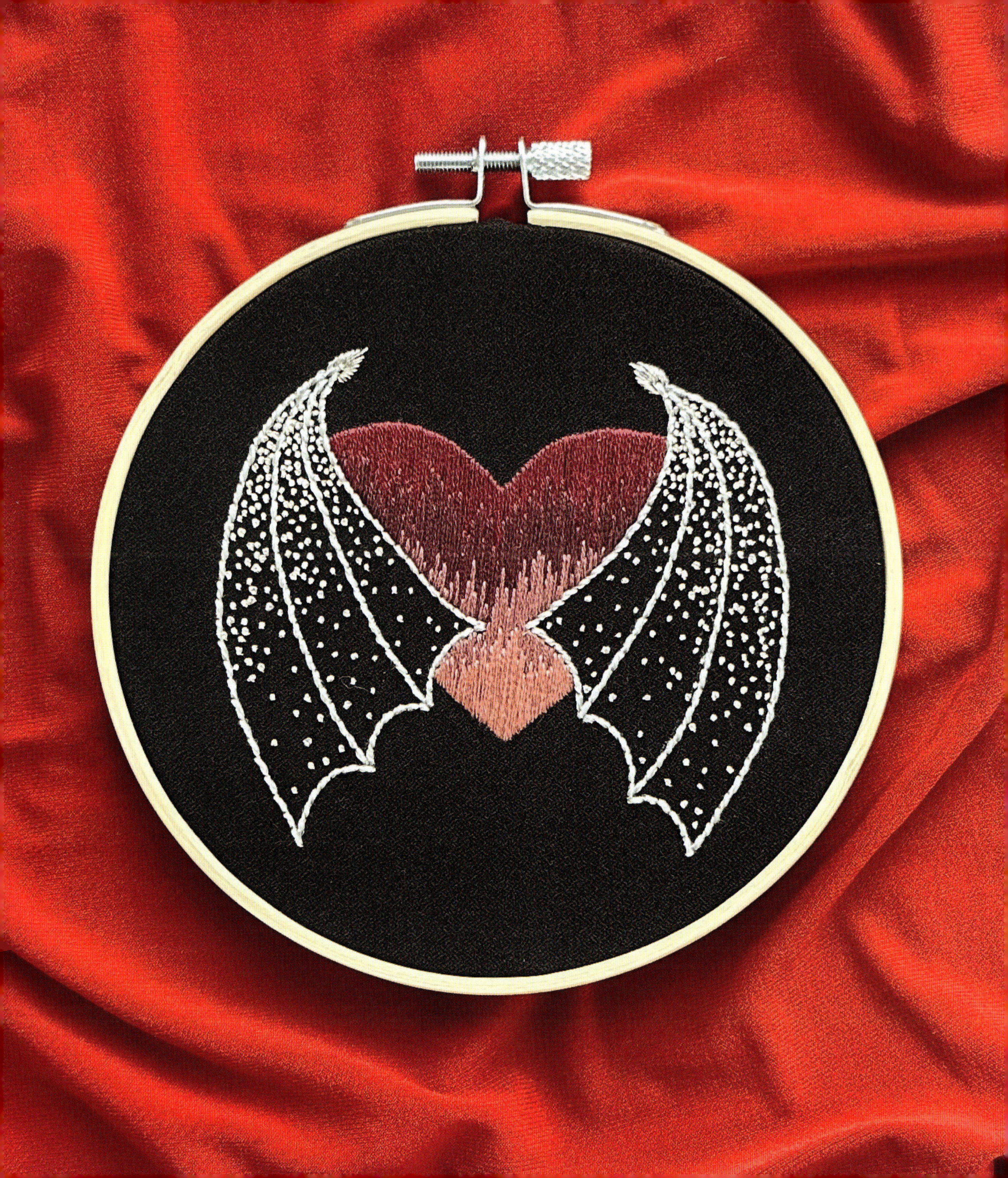

Wings of Desire

Bat wings curled around a heart … need we say more? This romantasy staple is for anyone who's fallen for a winged, brooding love interest who *definitely* has a tragic backstory. Dramatic? Yes. Over the top? Also, yes. But that's exactly why we love it.

SUPPLIES

5" (13 cm) Embroidery Hoop

Fabric

Fabric Scissors

Embroidery Needle

Embroidery Scissors

STITCHES

Whipped Backstitch (A): page 11

Satin Stitch (C): page 12

French Knots (D): page 12

Long and Short Stitch (F): page 13

THREADS

DMC Floss Colors

168

223

3726

3802

3865

D168

Note

Use three strands of floss throughout, except for D168, use one strand.

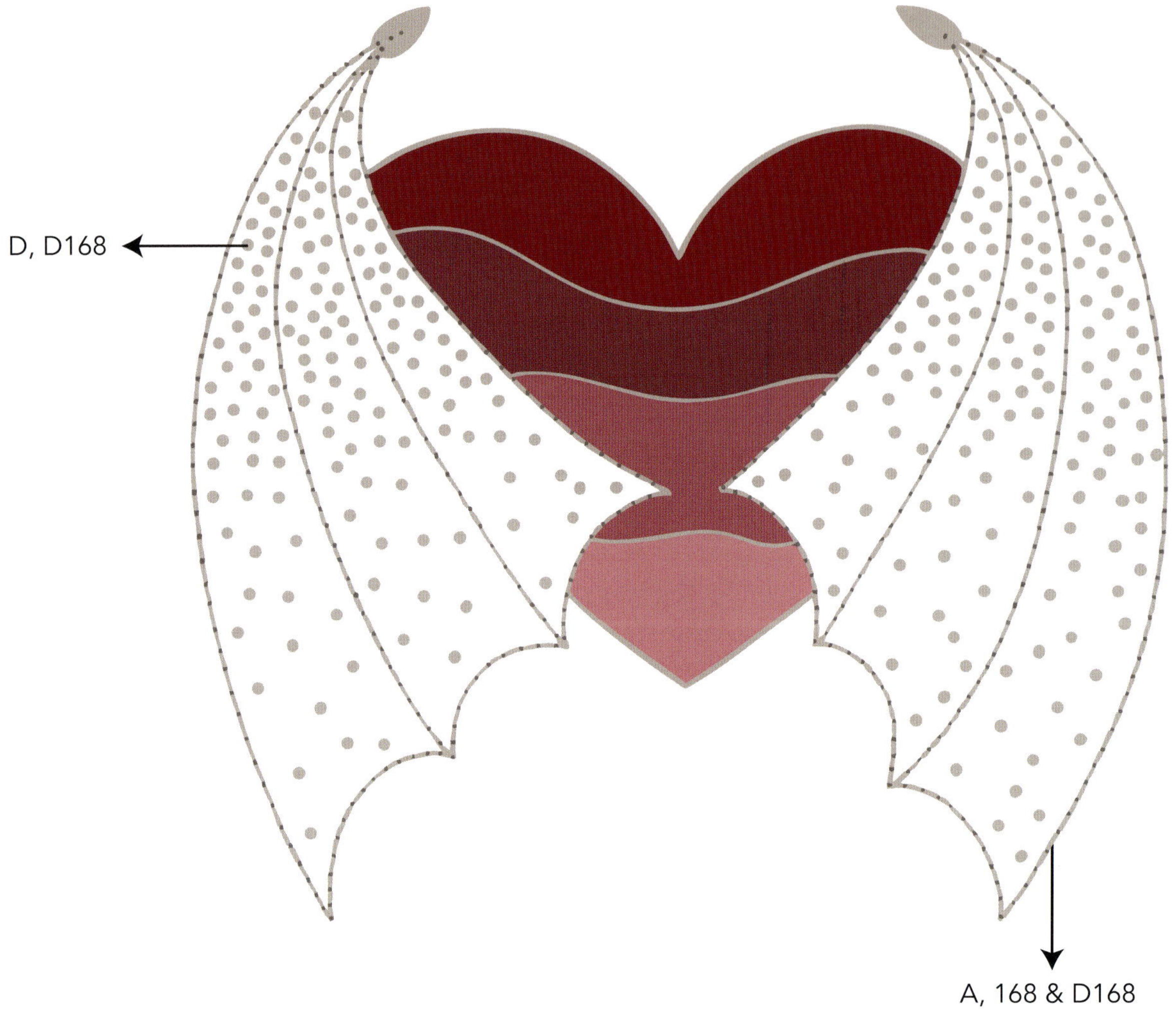

STITCH GUIDE

F	3865	F	223
F	3802	A	168
F	3726	C	D168

Heart and Wings template, page 105

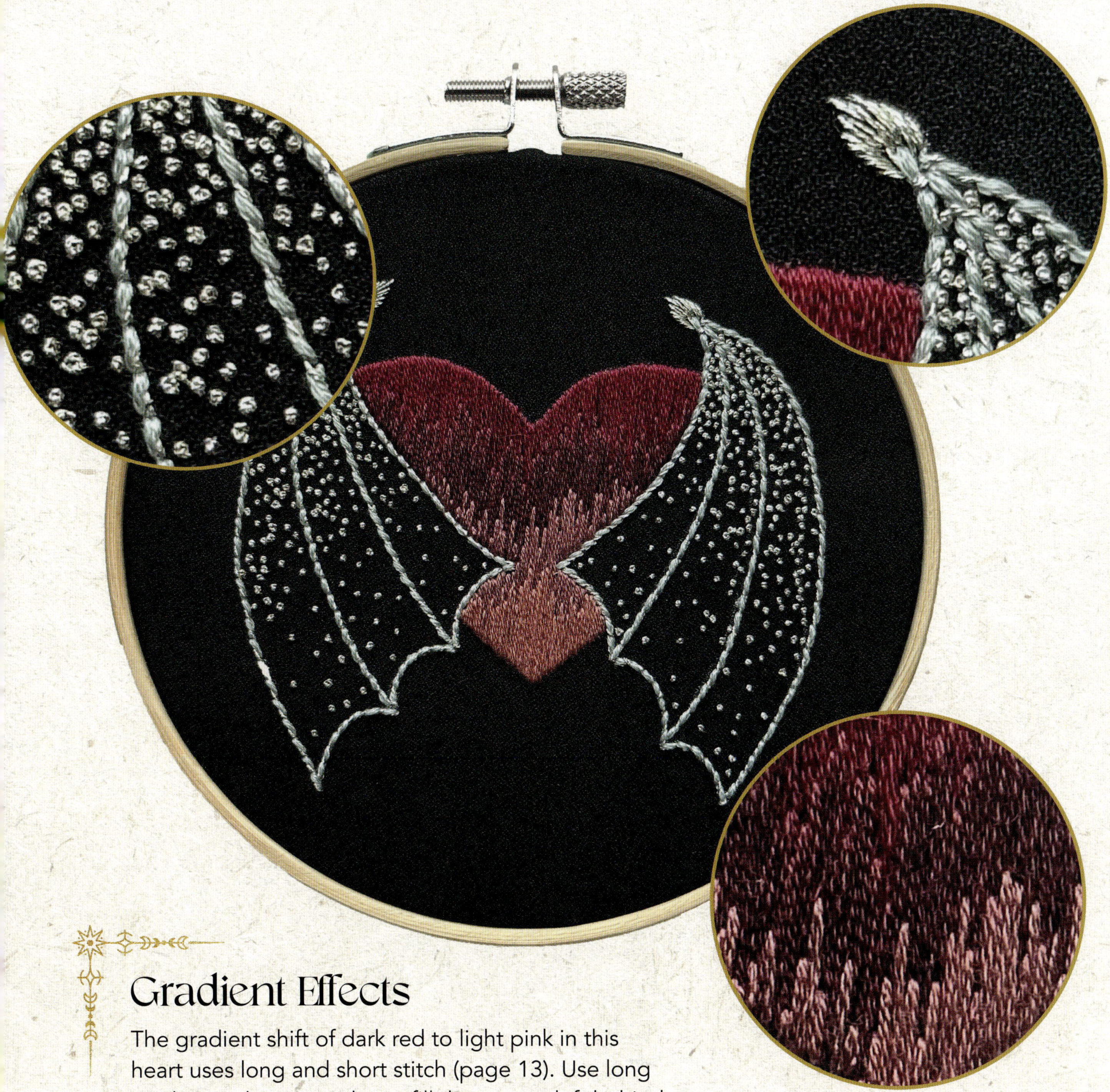

Gradient Effects

The gradient shift of dark red to light pink in this heart uses long and short stitch (page 13). Use long stitches in the next color to fill the spaces left behind by short stitches in the previous section.

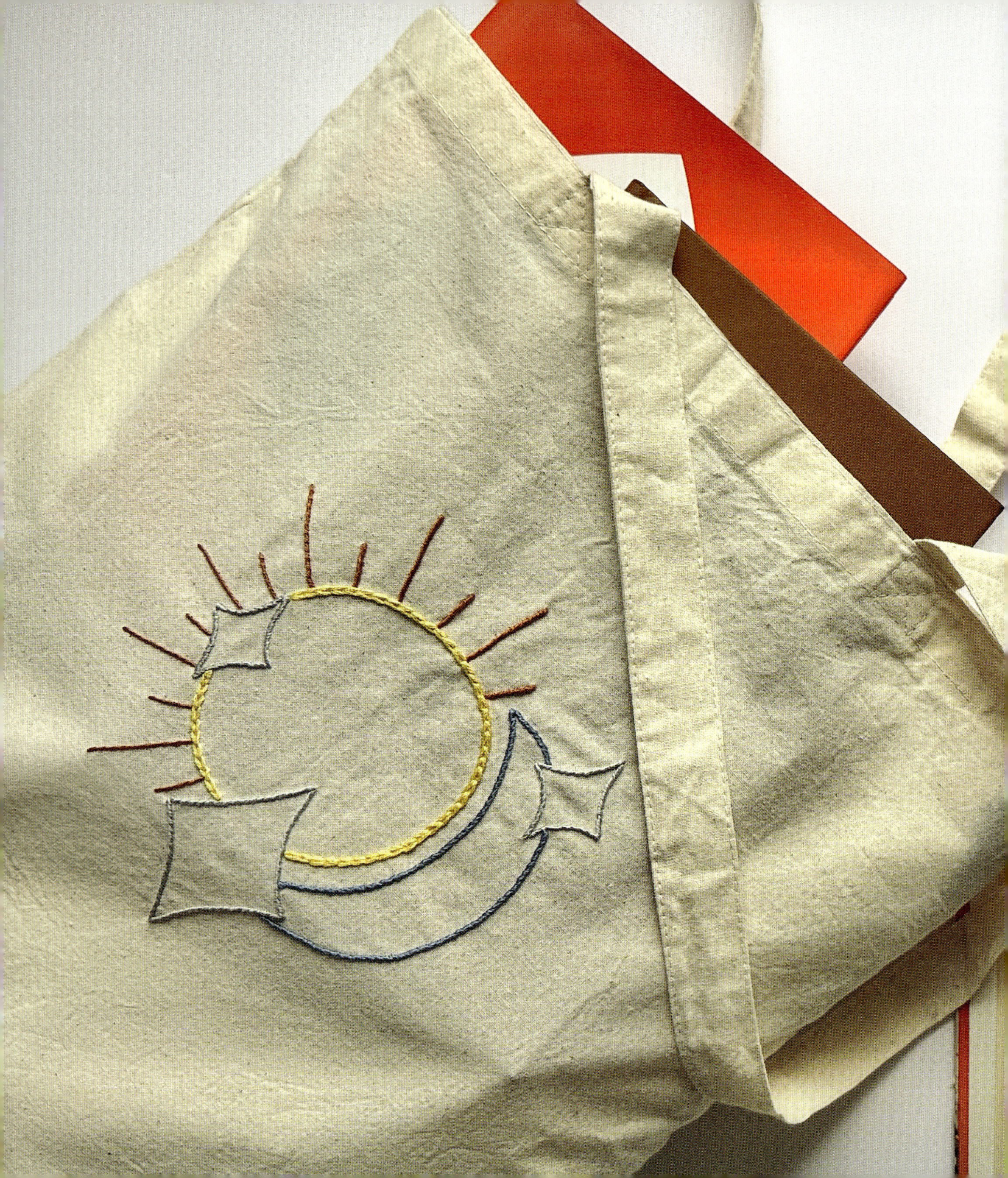

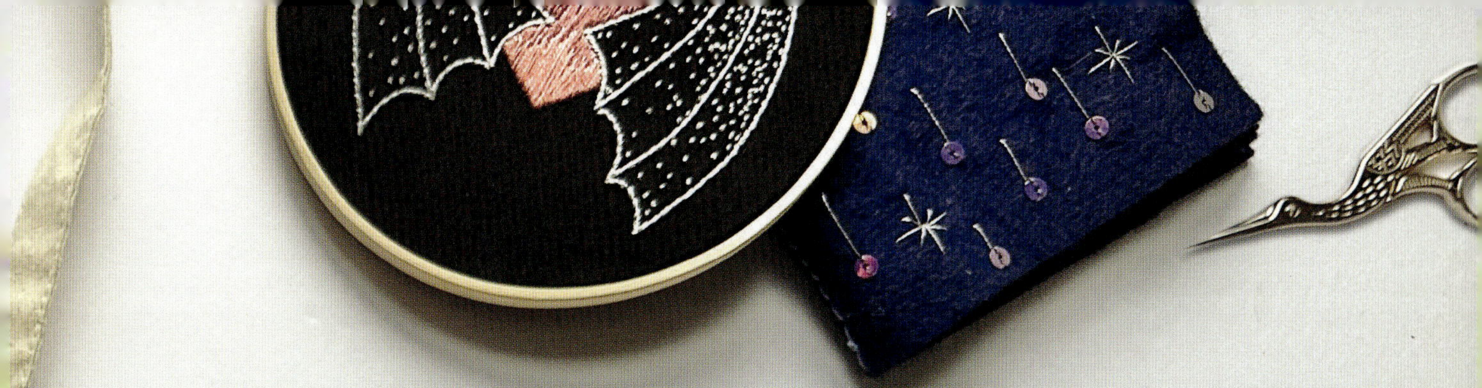

Out of the Hoop: Take Your Magic Everywhere

Embroidery doesn't have to stay in the frame. This chapter is all about letting your stitches roam onto tote bags, bookmarks, e-reader covers, and anywhere else you want to add a little romantasy sparkle. These patterns are designed to be versatile and adaptable, whether you're stitching on a canvas jacket, a cozy beanie, or a pillow that says *"yes, I read spicy fantasy in bed."*

Think of these projects as inspiration, not rules. Change the colors, add beads, skip pieces that don't speak to you. This is your adventure, and the embroidery should be as bold, soft, mysterious, or over-the-top as the stories you love.

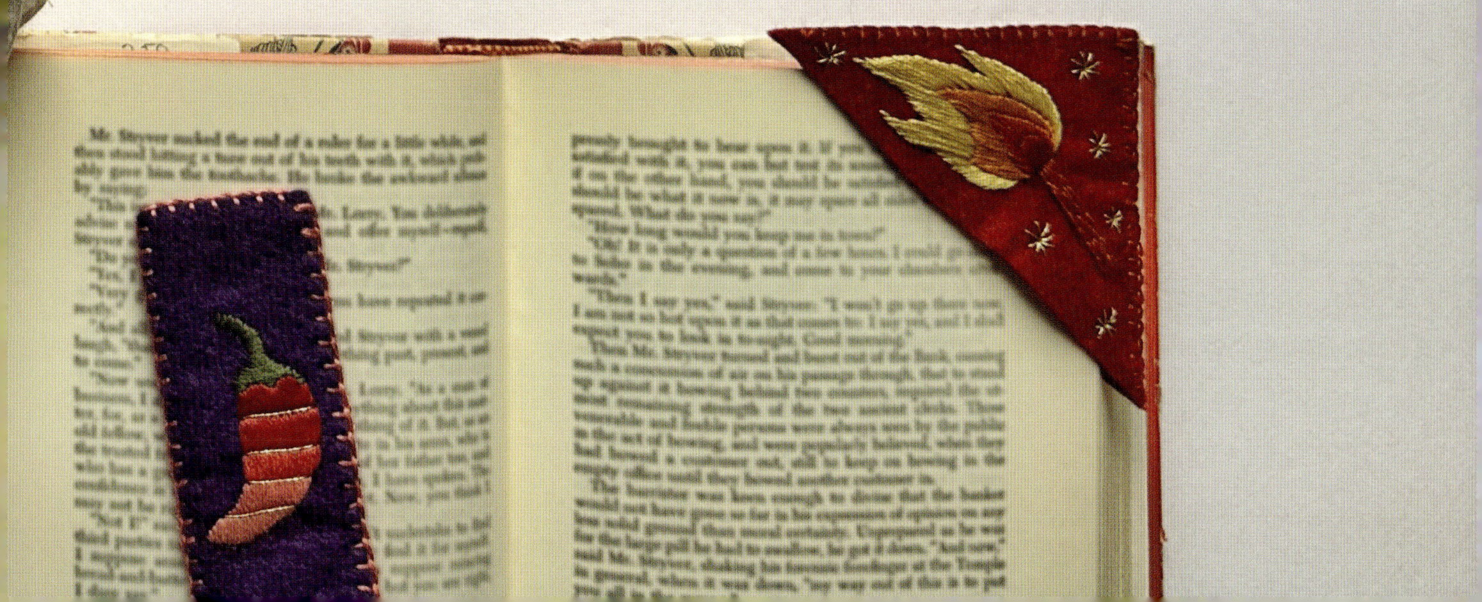

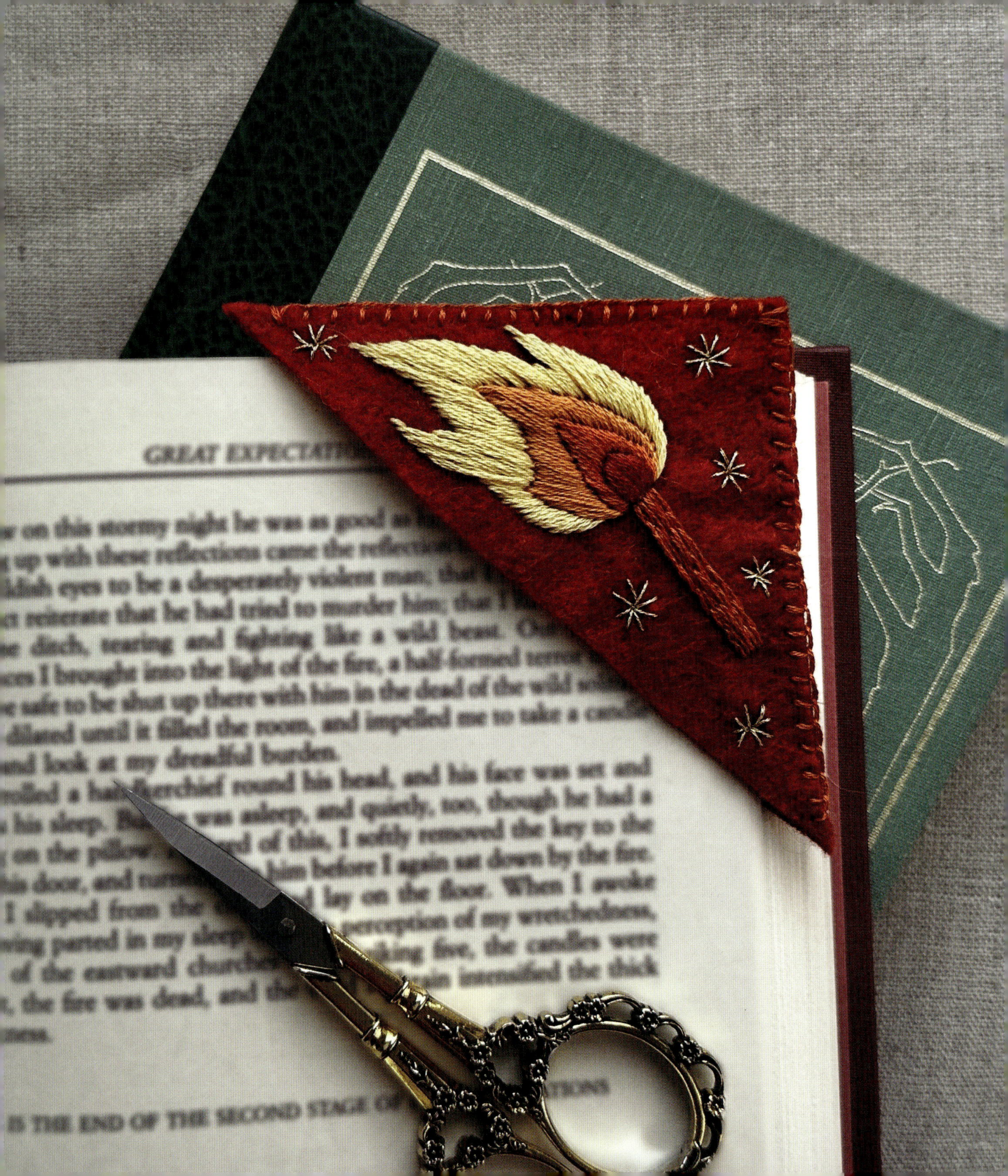

Slow Burn Bookmark

A single spark. That's how it starts. This felt corner bookmark features a stitched match. It's a simple, smoldering, and a *very* slow burn. Perfect for marking the page where your favorite couple almost kisses … for the fifth time. Let the tension simmer with every chapter you devour.

SUPPLIES

Felt Fabric

Fabric Scissors

Embroidery Needle

Embroidery Scissors

STITCHES

Satin Stitch (C): page 12

Straight Stitch (E): page 13

Long and Short Stitch (F): page 13

Blanket Stitch: page 15

THREADS

DMC Floss Colors

920

976

3777

3822

D3821

Note

Use all six strands of floss throughout, except for D3821, use one strand.

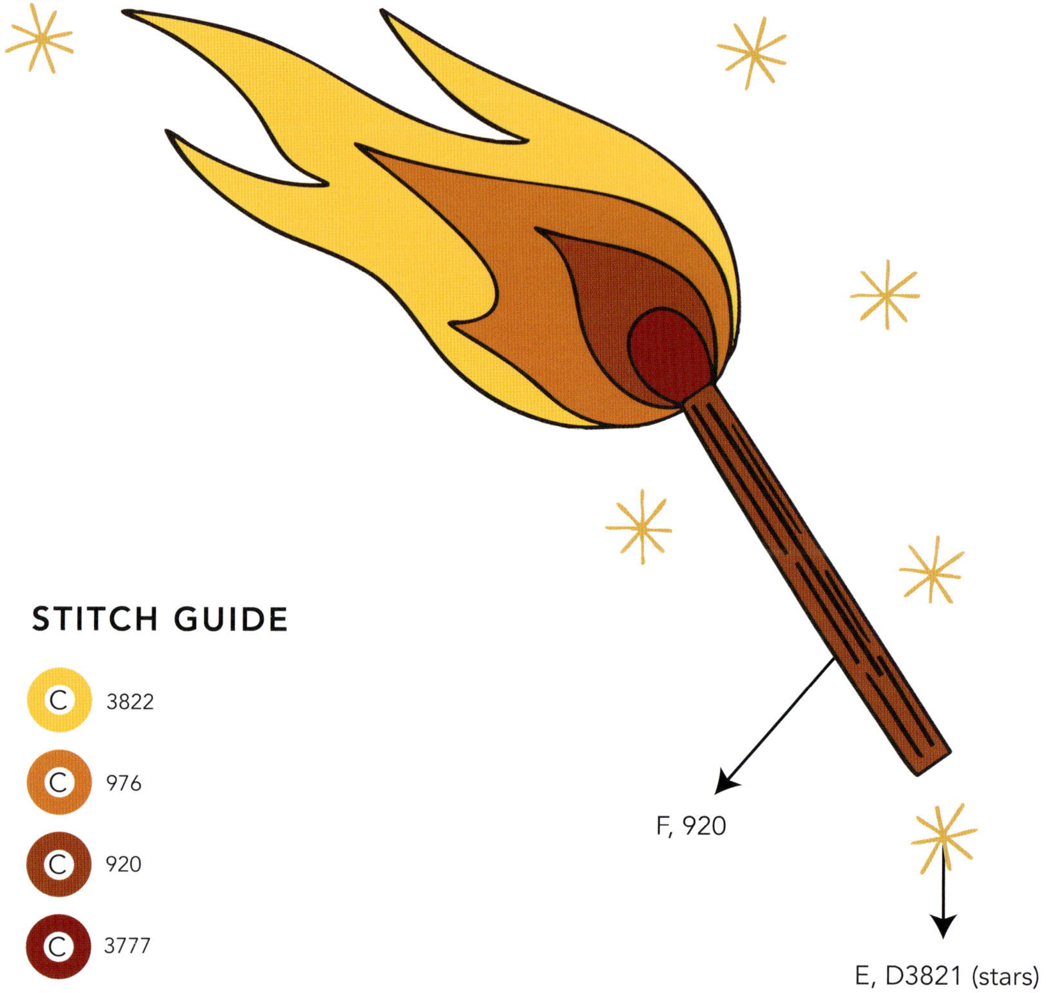

STITCH GUIDE

- C 3822
- C 976
- C 920
- C 3777
- F 920
- E D3821

Match template, page 109

1. Cut a square of felt with sides measuring about 3½" (7.5 cm). Cut diagonally across the square and set one triangle aside. Or you can cut to your desired size.

2. Transfer the Match template to your triangle of fabric and embroider according to the stitch diagram.

3. When stitching is complete, place the second triangle of felt behind the embroidered piece. Blanket stitch (page 15) the edges of the felt together with DMC 920.

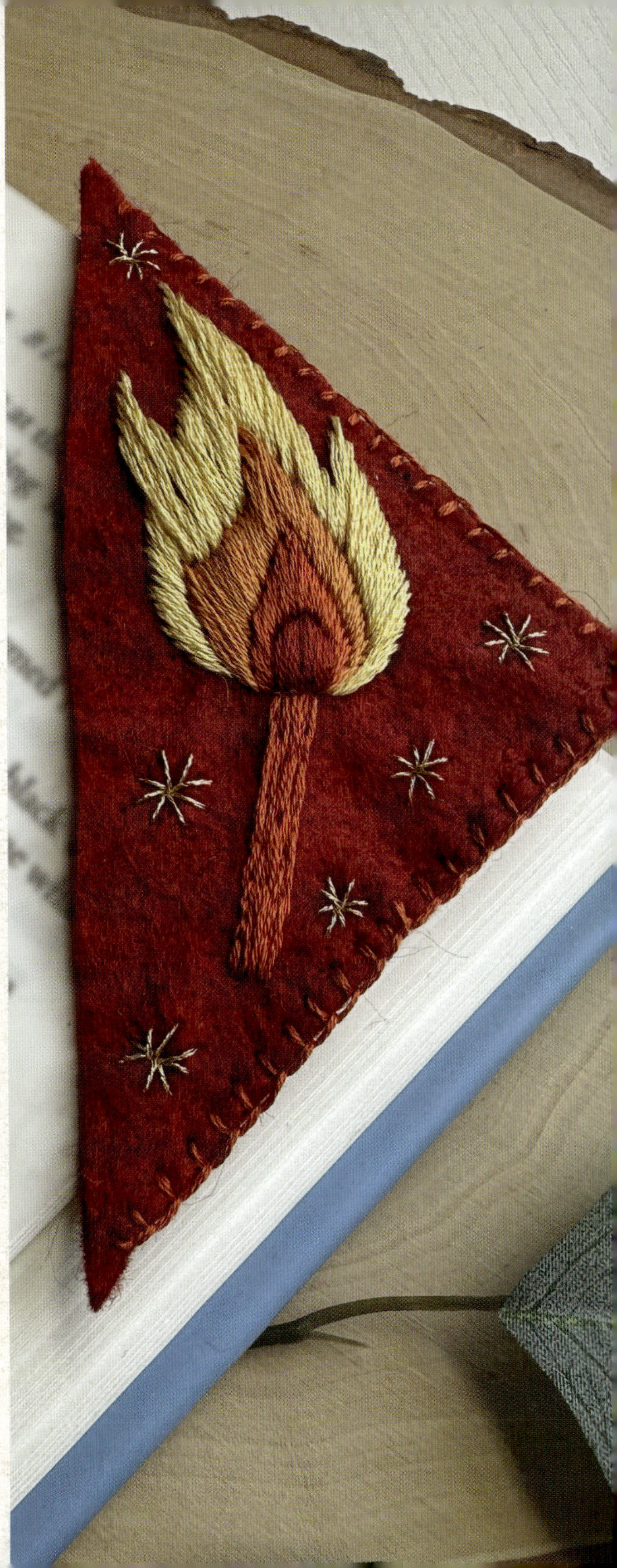

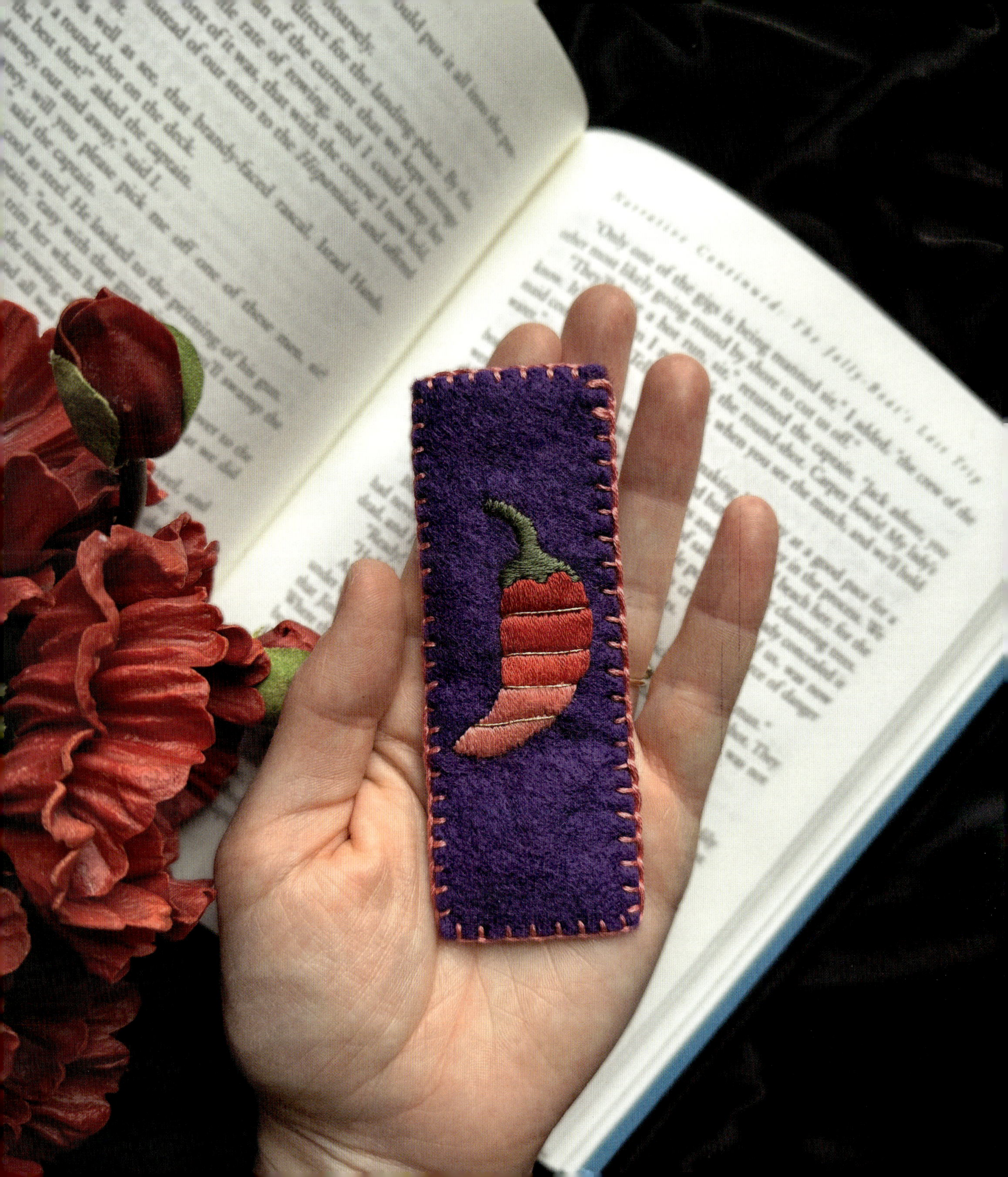

Spicy Pepper Bookmark

Not all romances are created equal; some bring the heat. This stitchable bookmark includes a cheeky pepper rating scale, from "tame and sweet" to "on-fire, read with caution." A must-have for your bedside TBR stack (and your stitch stash), fill the pepper accordingly.

SUPPLIES

Felt Fabric

Fabric Scissors

Embroidery Needle

Embroidery Scissors

STITCHES

Satin Stitch (C): page 12

Straight Stitch (E): page 13

Blanket Stitch: page 15

THREADS

DMC Floss Colors

760

816

3051

3821

3832

3833

D3821

Note

Use all six strands of floss throughout, except for D3821, use one strand.

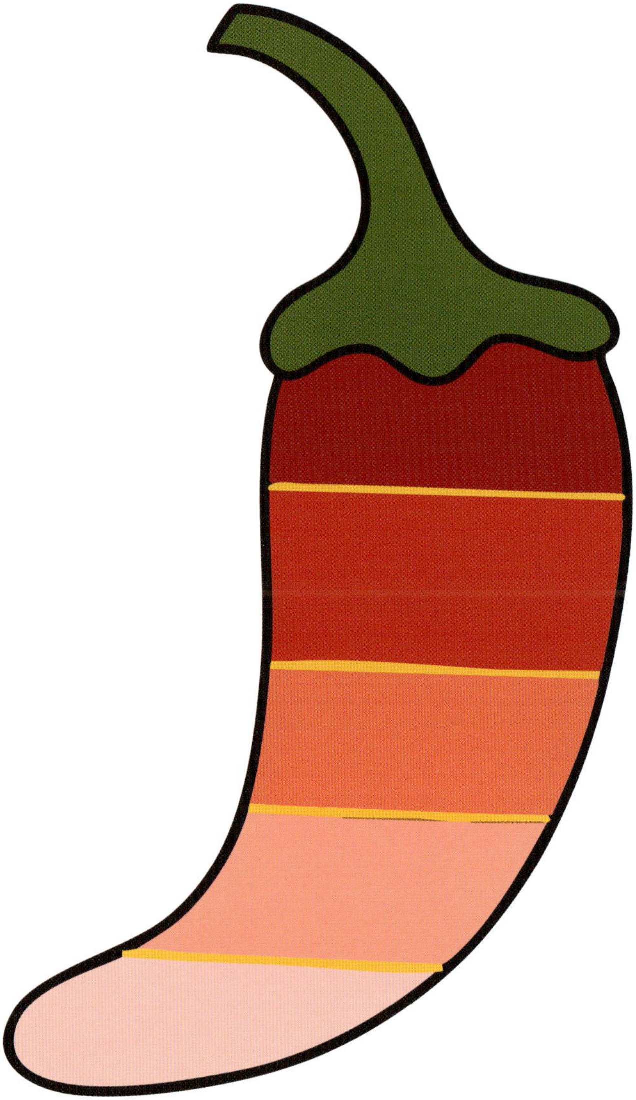

STITCH GUIDE

- C 816
- C 3821
- C 3832
- C 3833
- C 760
- C 3051
- E D3821

Spicy Pepper template, page 106

1. Cut two rectangles of felt sheet to about 1½" × 4¼" (3 × 10.5 cm), or your desired size. Set one rectangle aside.

2. Transfer the Spicy Pepper template to your rectangle of fabric and embroider according to the stitch diagram.

3. When stitching is complete, place the second rectangle of felt behind the embroidered piece. Blanket stitch (page 15) the edges of the felt together with DMC 3833.

Turn Up the Heat

For an even spicier bookmark, repeat the template multiple times on the felt. For less spice, embroider just a few sections of a single pepper.

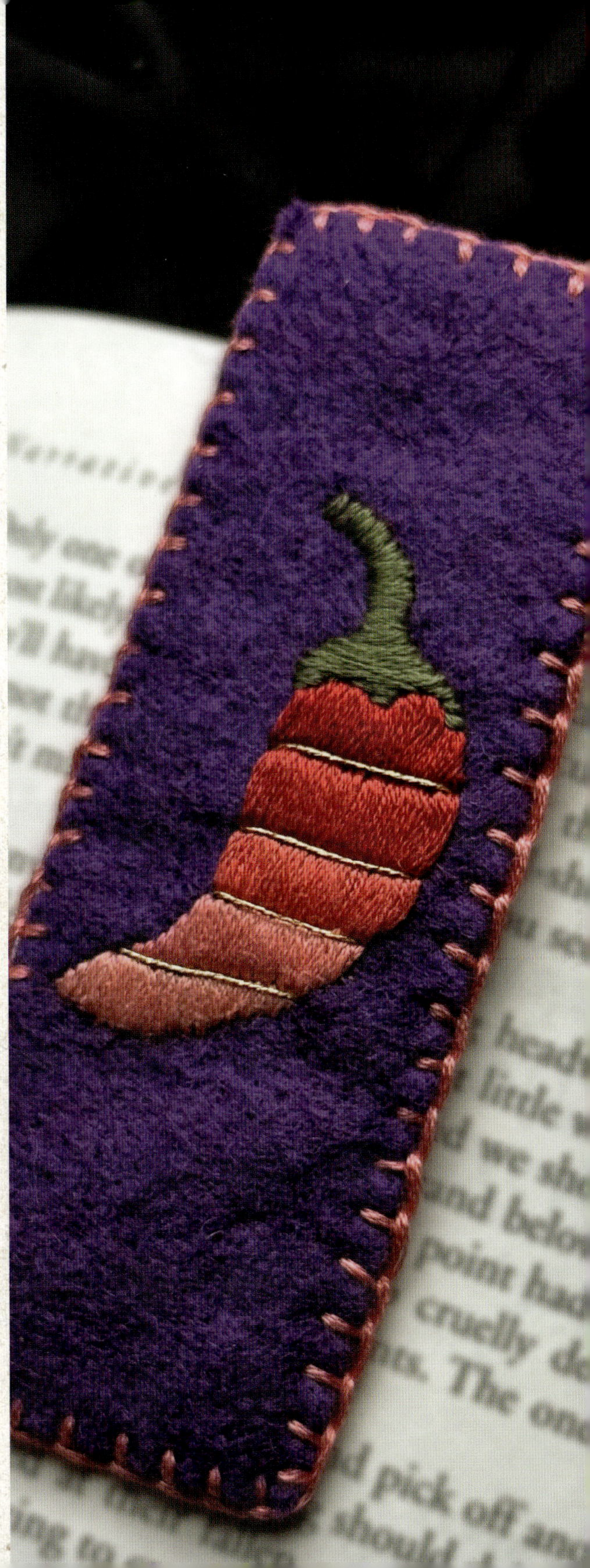

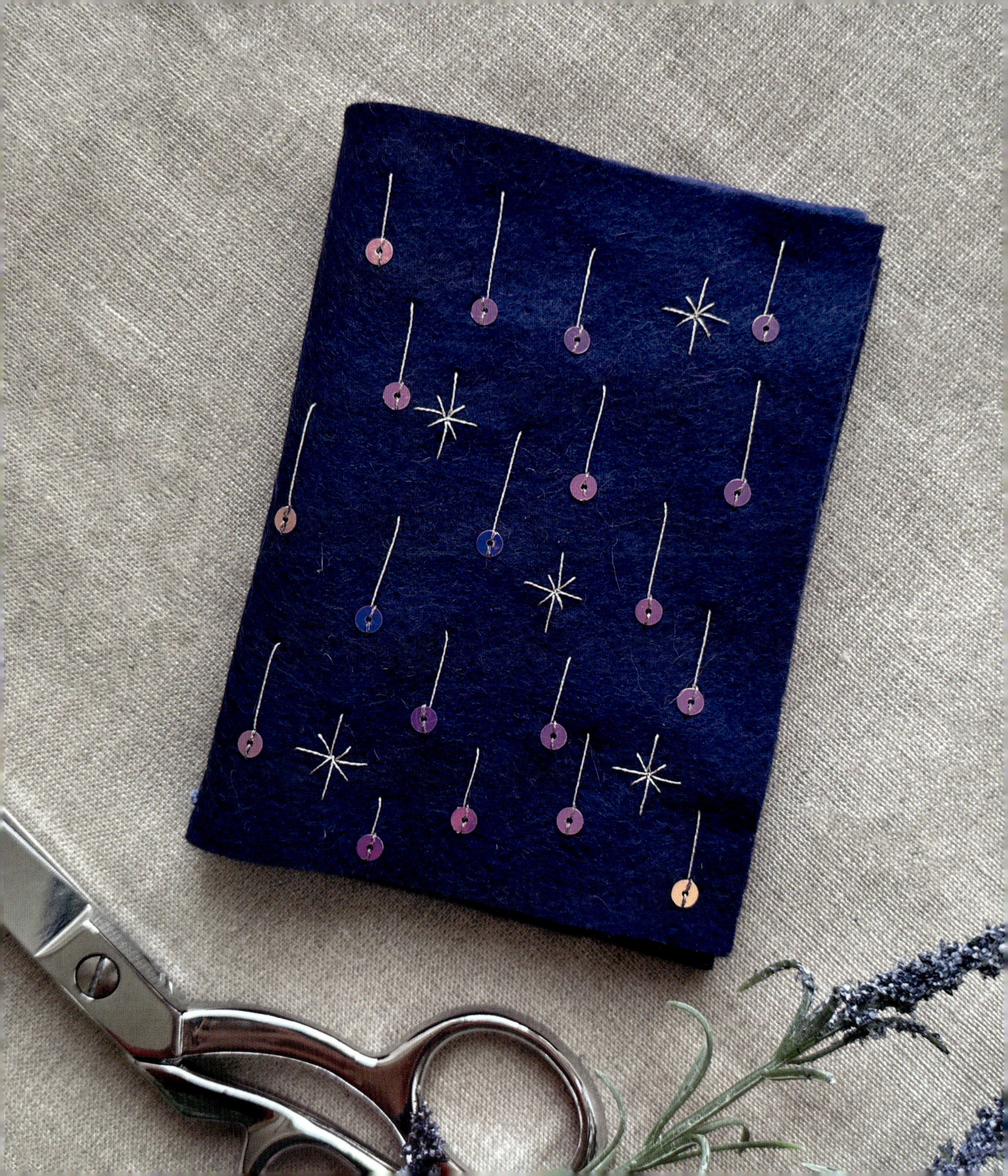

Starfall Needle Book

Keep your needles safe and your imagination starry-eyed. This celestial needle book design is inspired by one of romantasy's most iconic skies—complete with a stitched Starfall moment. It's equal parts practical and dreamy, perfect for readers who like a little magic with their notions.

SUPPLIES

2 Pieces of Felt Fabric (navy and light blue)

Fabric Scissors

Embroidery Needle

Embroidery Scissors

4 mm Sequins (silver)

STITCHES

Straight Stitch (E): page 13

Backstitch: page 11

THREADS

DMC Floss Colors

D168

Note

Use one strand of floss throughout.

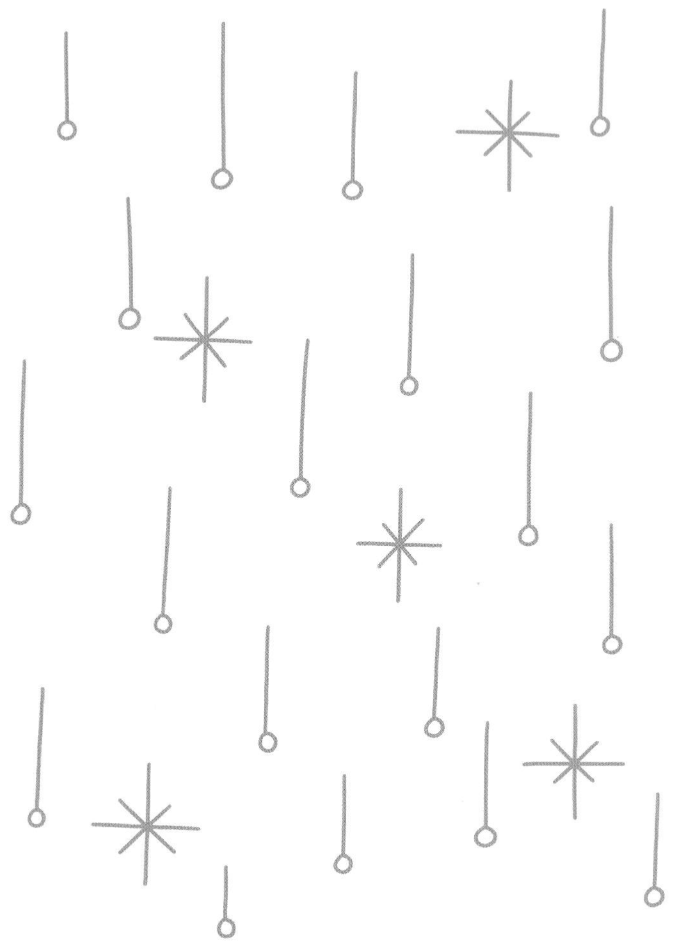

STITCH GUIDE

E D168

Sequins

Starfall template, page 109

1. For the cover of the needle book, cut a piece of felt fabric to 9" × 6" (23 × 15 cm).

2. Transfer the Starfall template to the front right half of the cover fabric and embroider according to the stitch diagram.

3. Cut two to three more pieces of felt fabric about ¼" (.5 cm) smaller than the cover piece. These will become the pages in the needle book.

4. Layer the pages on the wrong side of the embroidered cover and center.

5. Stitching through all the layers (cover and pages), backstitch the center spine of the needle book, securing each end with a clean knot.

6. Fold the book in half along the spine just stitched and finger press the edge to hold the shape.

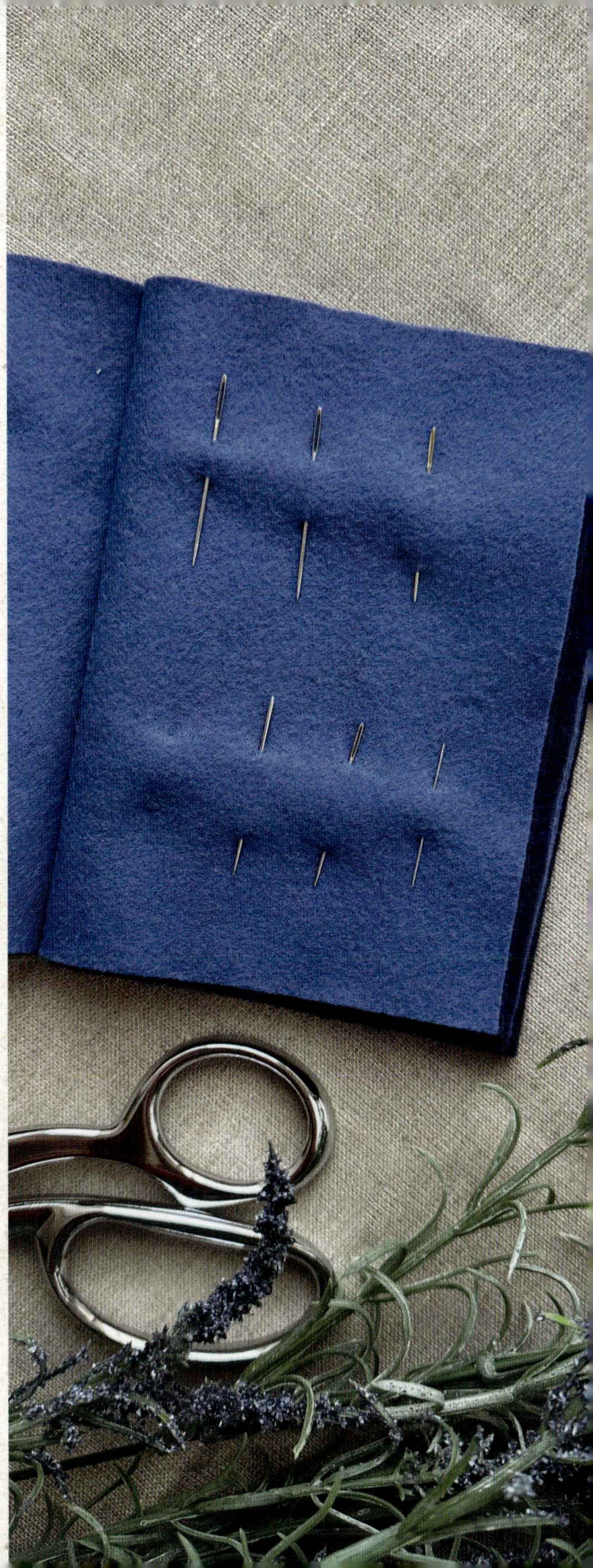

Easily Customizable

This needle book is very easy to resize! Just make the cover rectangle larger or smaller to suit your needs. Then, sketch the Starfall design on the front section. It's as easy as that.

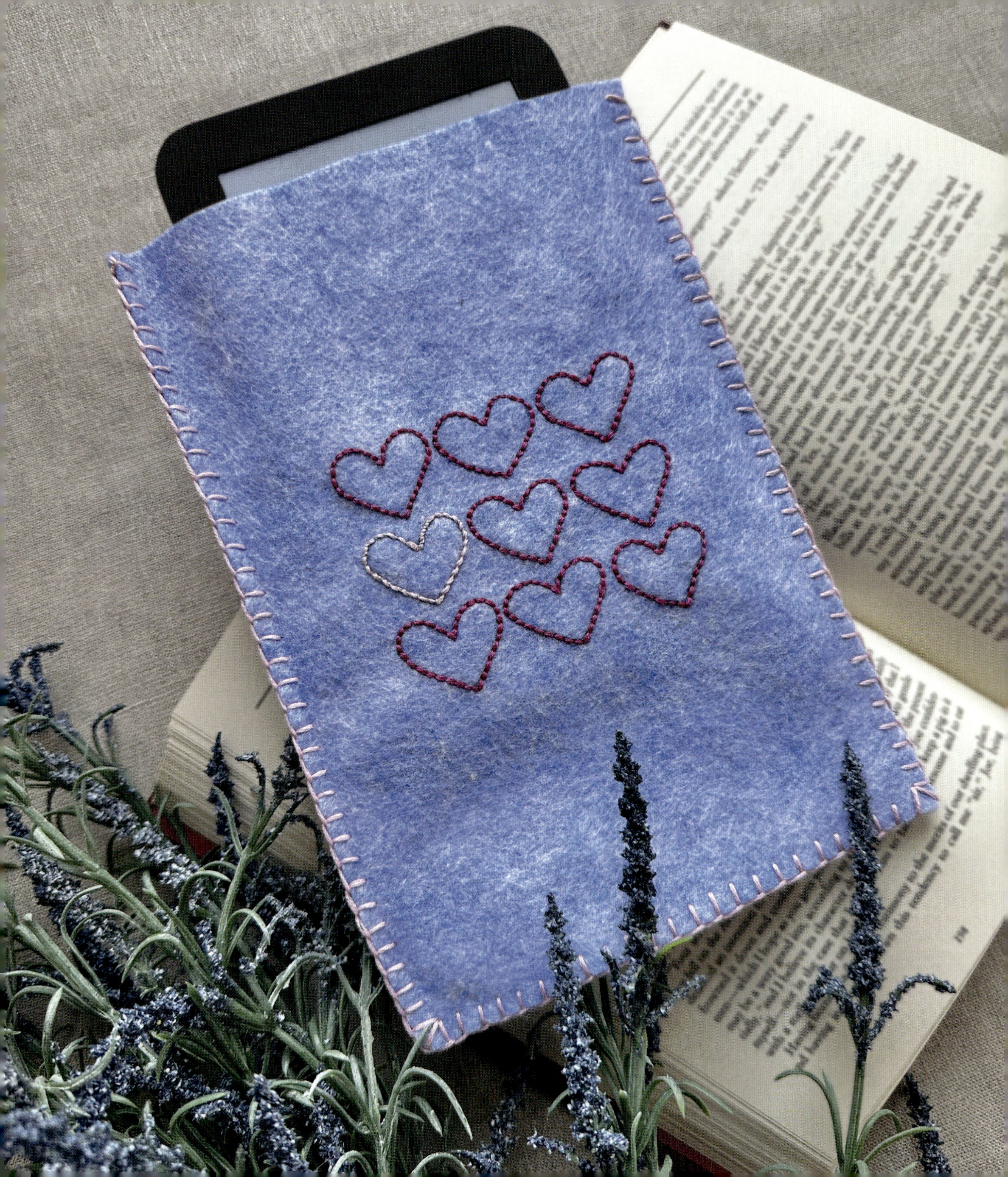

Hearts E-Reader Cover

This e-reader case features a stitched grid of hearts—soft, sweet, and maybe suspiciously shadowy. Showcase your love of all things romantic and happy (eventual) endings. Want to be bold? Add a stitched line down the middle for those morally gray choices. This cover is perfect for protecting your digital book boyfriends.

SUPPLIES

Felt Fabric

Fabric Scissors

Embroidery Needle

Embroidery Scissors

STITCHES

Whipped Backstitch (A): page 11 (optional)

Backstitch (B): page 11

Blanket Stitch: page 15

THREADS

DMC Floss Colors

917

3689

D168 (optional)

Note

Use all six strands of floss throughout, except for D168, use one strand.

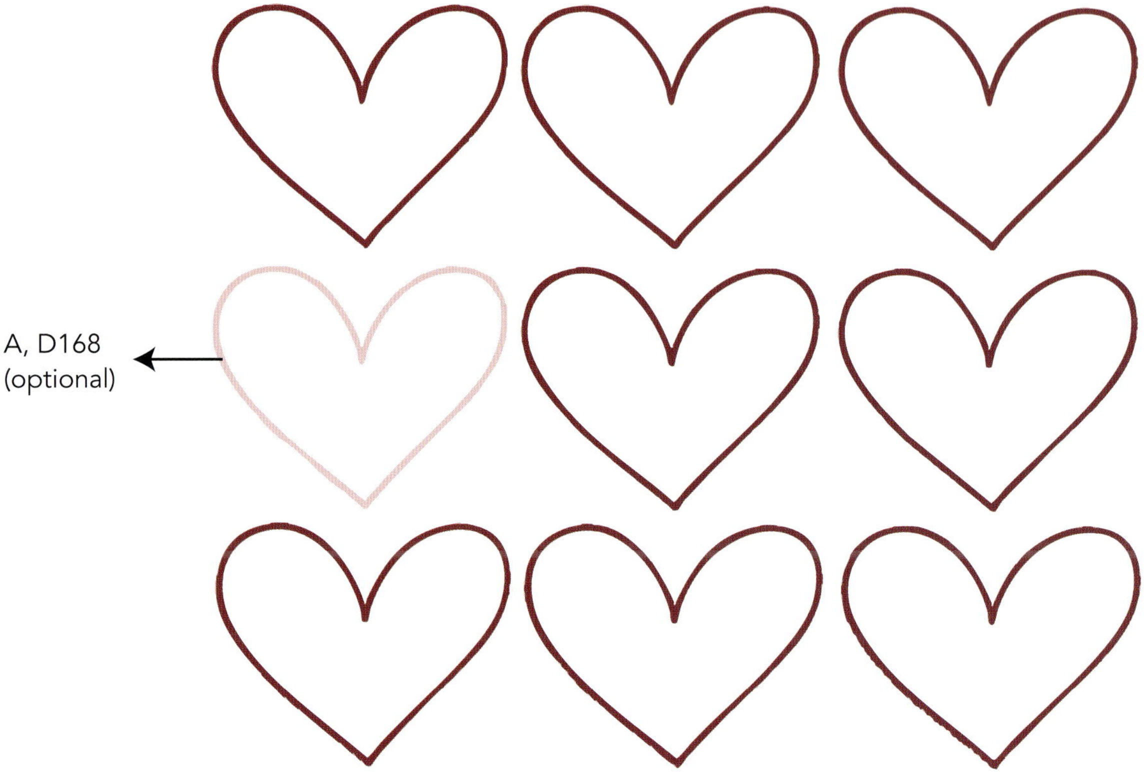

STITCH GUIDE

A 3689

B 917

Hearts template, page 109

1. Cut two pieces of felt fabric about ½" (1 cm) larger than your e-reader. Set one piece aside.

2. Transfer the Hearts template to the felt fabric and embroider according to the stitch diagram.

3. When stitching is complete, place the second rectangle of felt behind the embroidered piece. Blanket stitch (page 15) three edges of the felt together with DMC 3689. Leaving one side open allows you to slide your e-reader into the case.

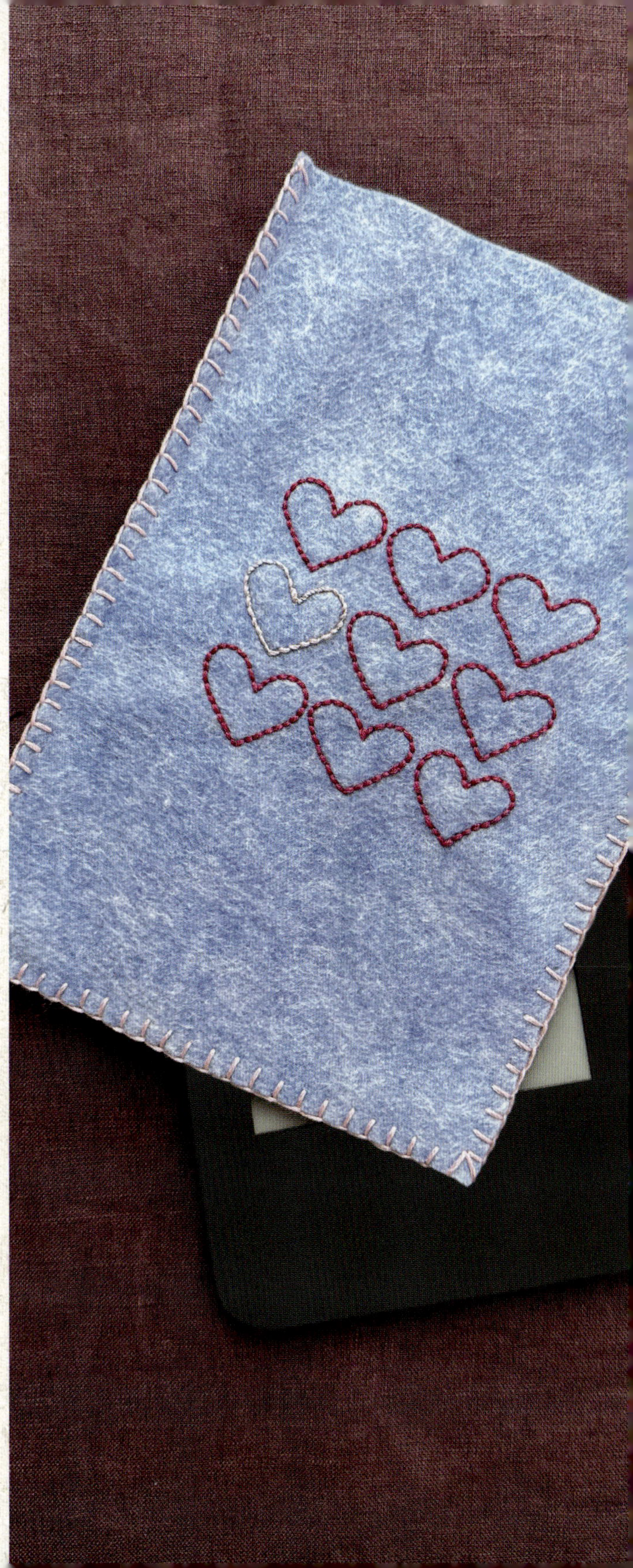

A Bit of Simmer

For the light pink heart, add an element of sparkle with D168 and whipped backstitch.

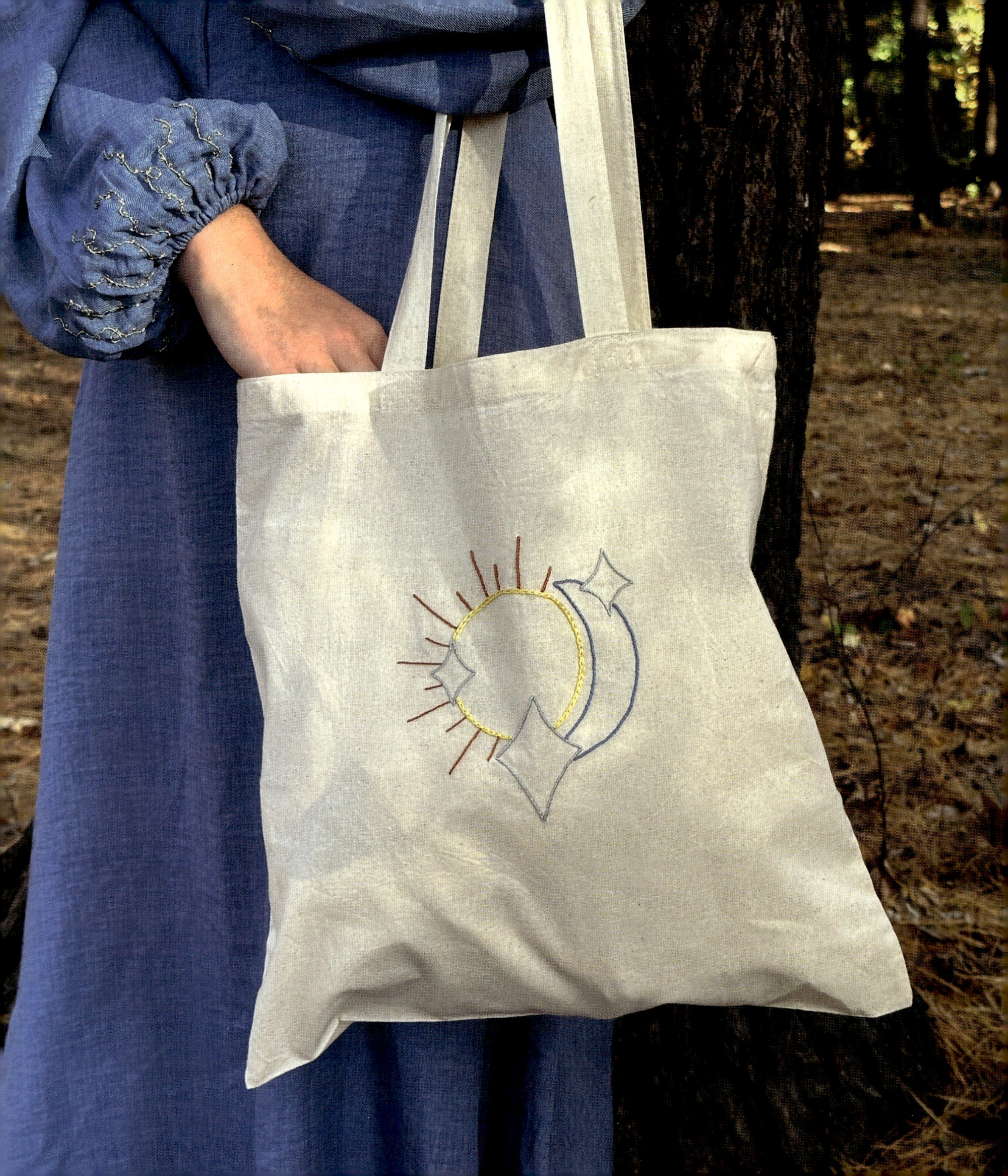

Sun & Moon Canvas Tote

Inspired by cosmic duality and romantasy's favorite opposites-attract energy, these sun-and-moon embroidery motifs are meant to shine wherever you take them. Try them on a canvas tote or go rogue and stitch them on a jacket, hoodie, or anything else that deserves a little celestial drama.

SUPPLIES

Canvas Tote

Embroidery Needle

Embroidery Scissors

Iron-on Backing (optional)

STITCHES

Whipped Backstitch (A): page 11

Chain Stitch (I): page 14

Blanket Stitch: page 15

THREADS

DMC Floss Colors

168

301

322

726

Note

Use all six strands of floss throughout.

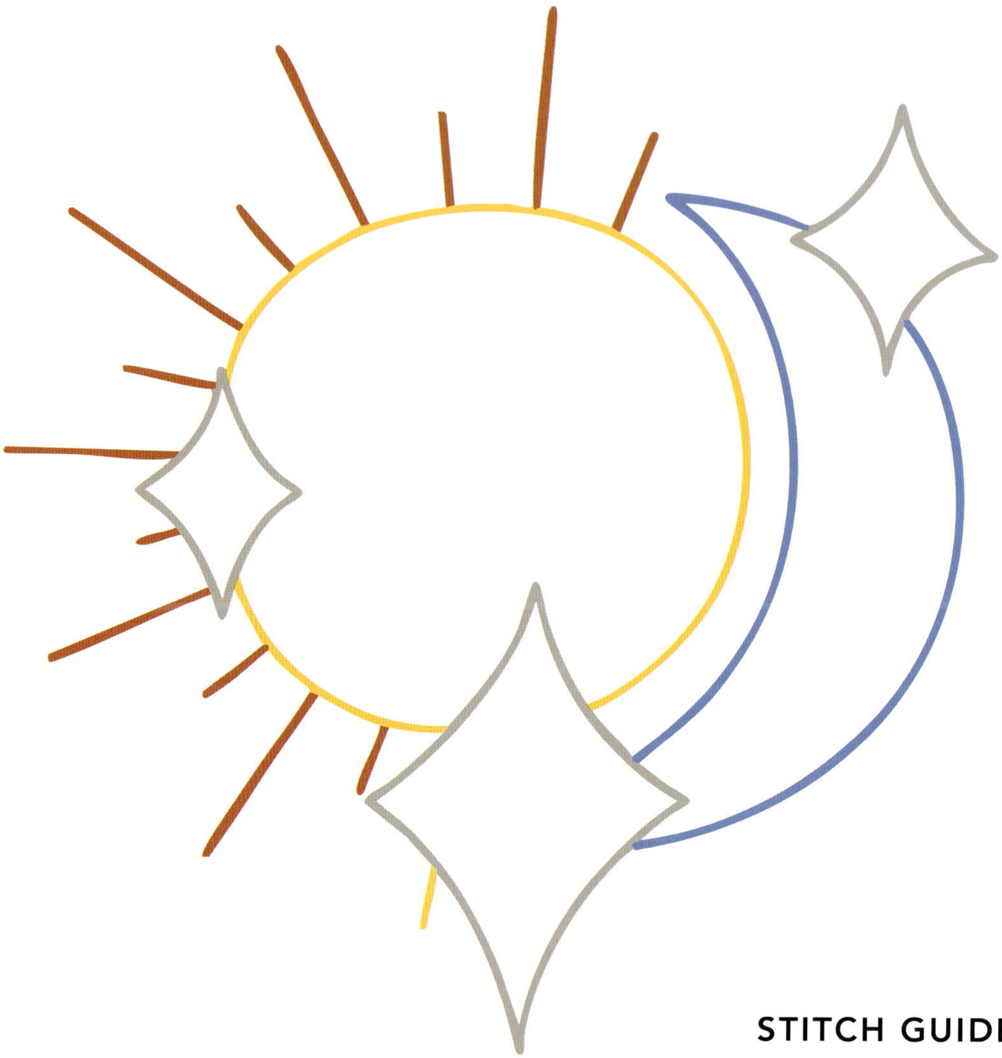

Sun, Moon, and Stars template, page 107

STITCH GUIDE

Stitch	Color
I	726
A	301
A	322
A	168

1. Transfer the Sun, Moons, and Stars template to your canvas tote.

2. Embroider according to the stitch diagram.

3. Optional: To protect your stitches from the wear and tear they'll receive as books pass in and out of your bag, add iron-on backing to cover the back side of the embroidery.

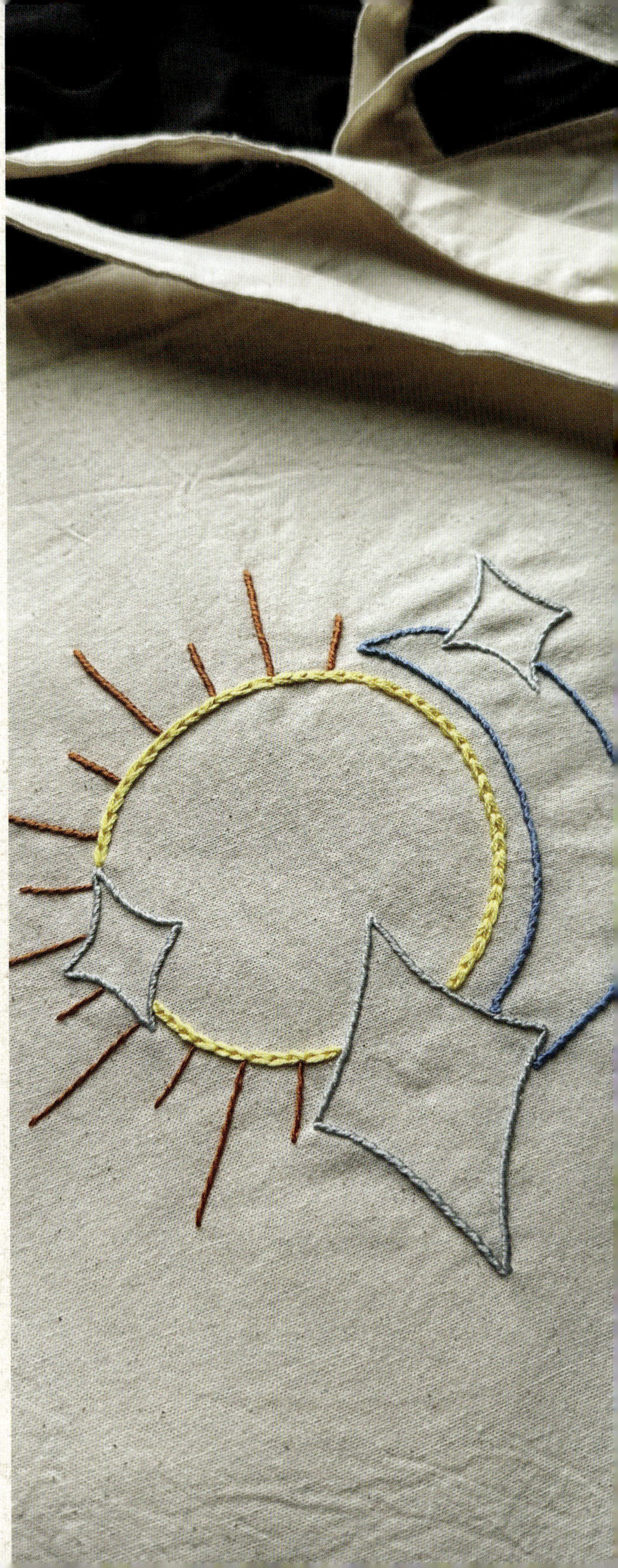

Templates

Every embroidery project is unique! Use the QR code provided to download printable templates that you can size up or down to suit your project. You can also use the PDF download to transfer patterns using the transfer methods outlined on page 9.

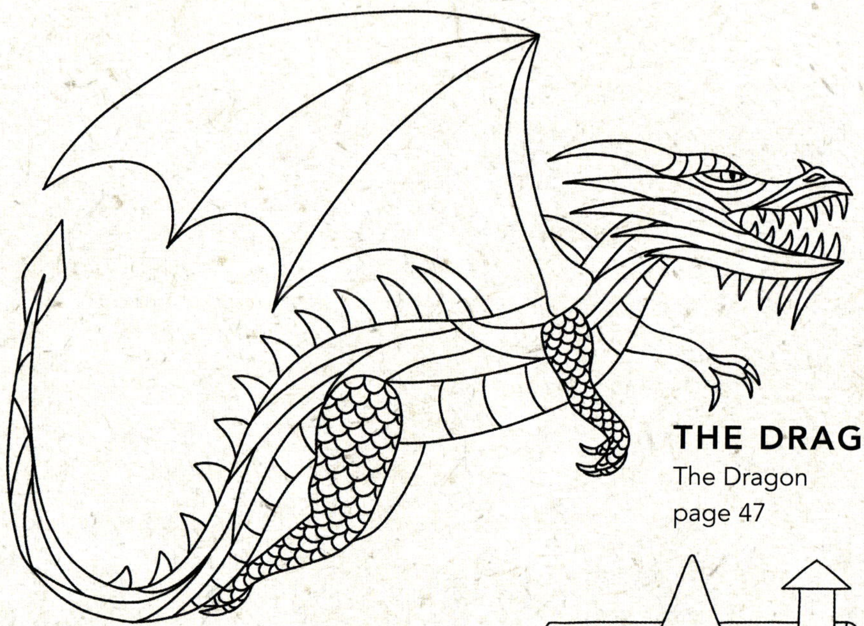

THE DRAGON

The Dragon
page 47

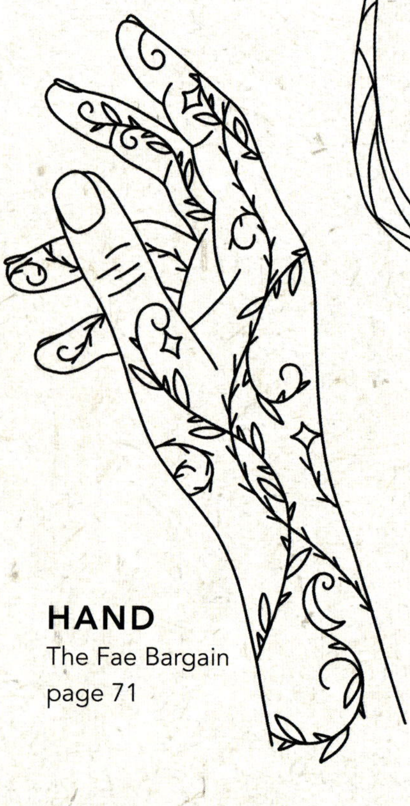

HAND

The Fae Bargain
page 71

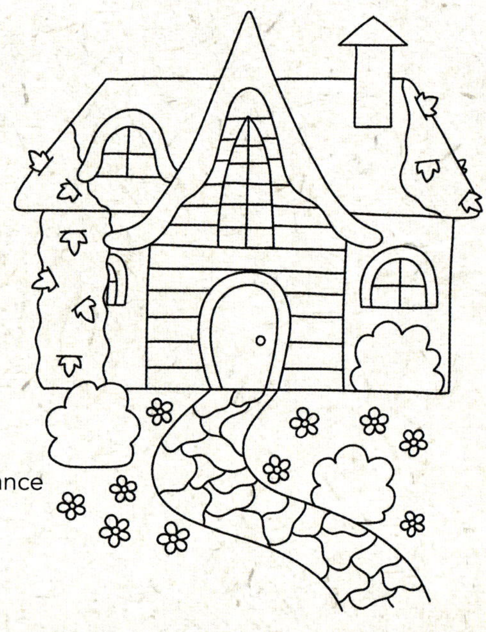

COTTAGE

Cottagecore Romance
page 39

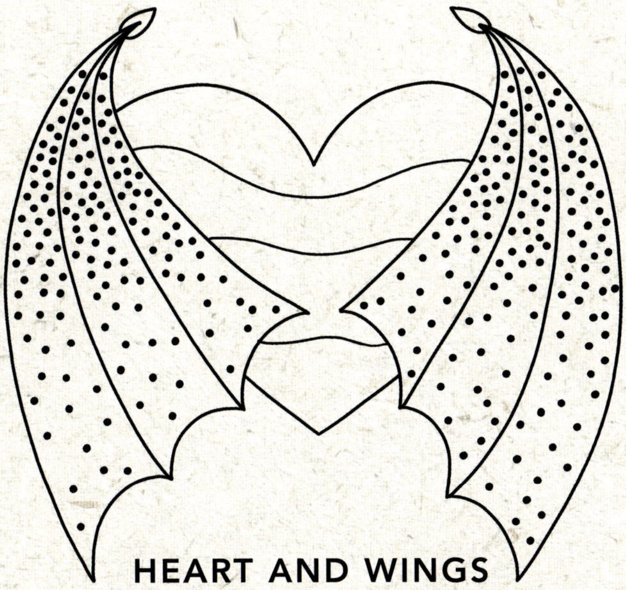

HEART AND WINGS
Wings of Desire
page 79

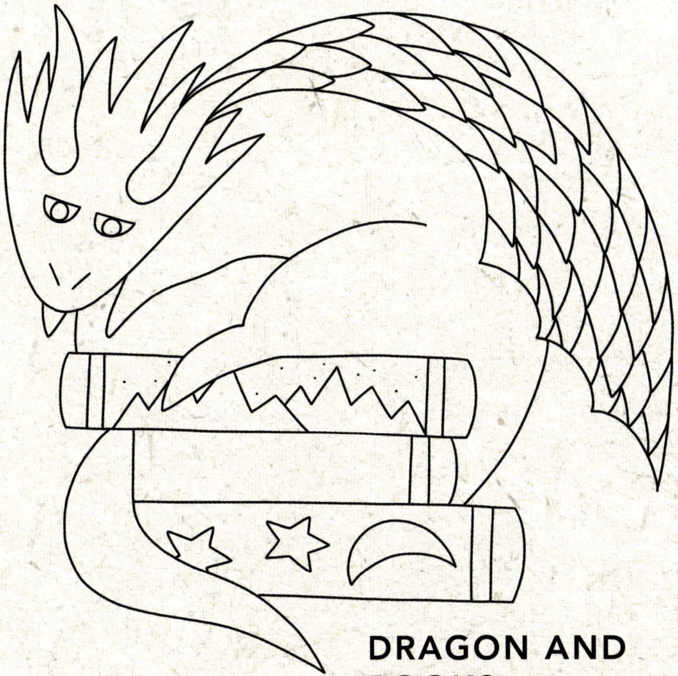

DRAGON AND BOOKS
Book Dragon's Hoard
page 31

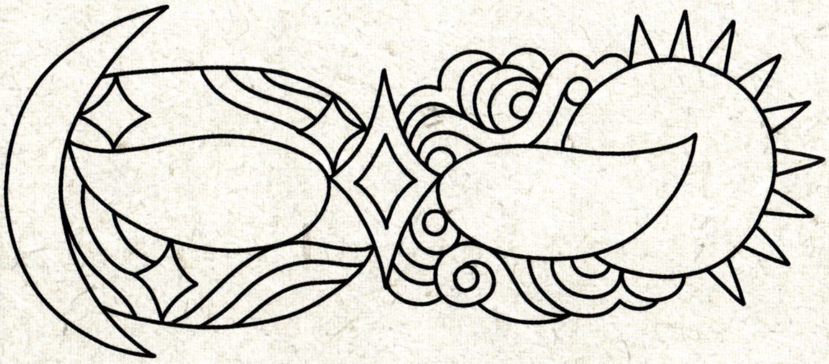

MASK
Masquerade Mystery
page 63

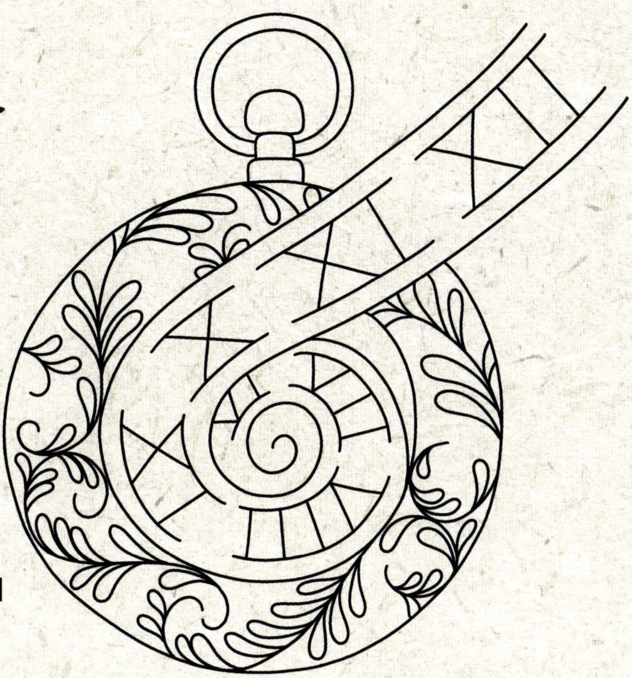

POCKET WATCH
Time Travel Love
page 43

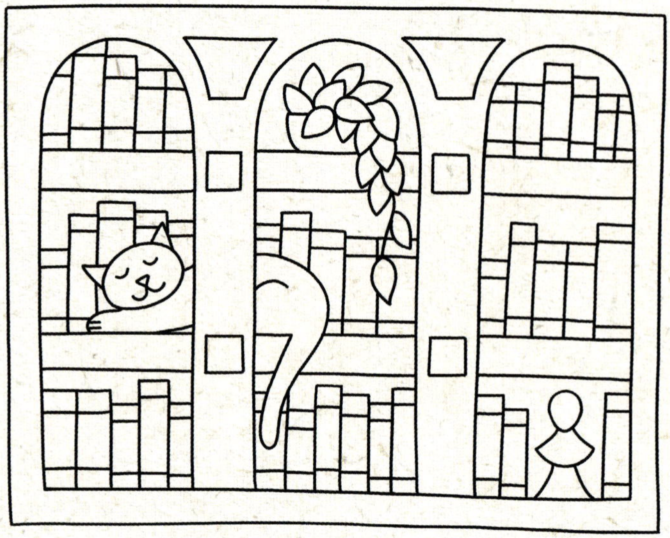

LIBRARY SHELVES
The Library Cat
page 51

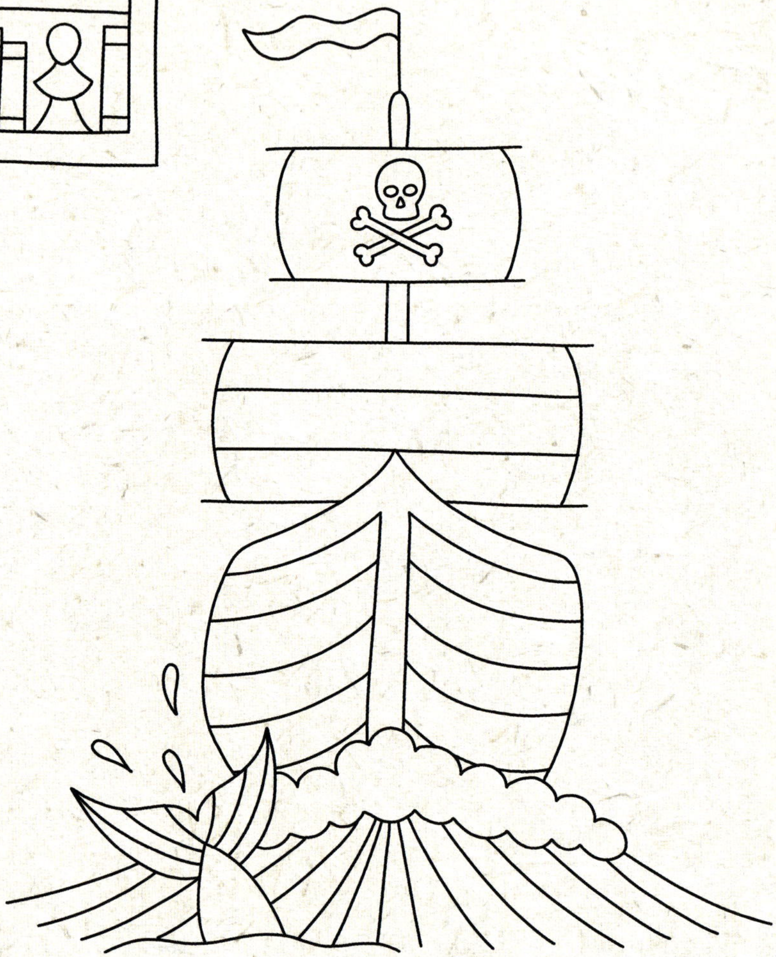

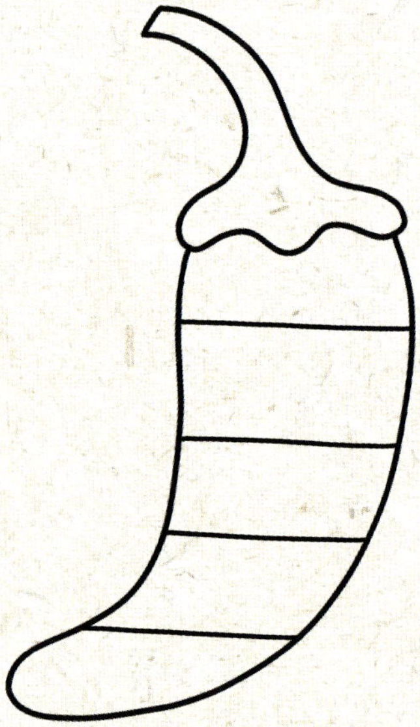

SPICY PEPPER
Spicy Pepper Bookmark
page 89

PIRATE SHIP
Sirens & Sails
page 35

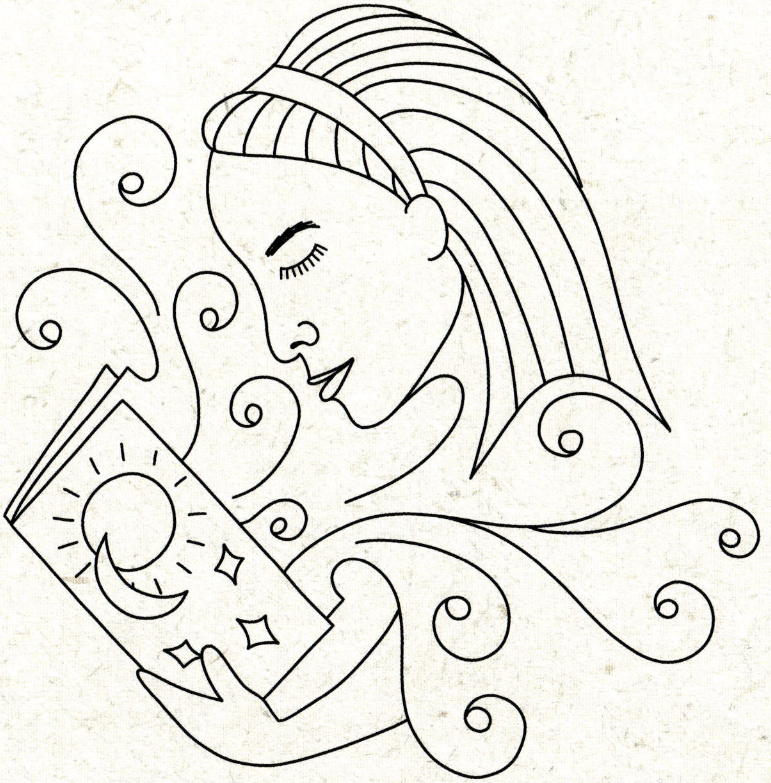

INK DRINKER
Ink Drinker
page 55

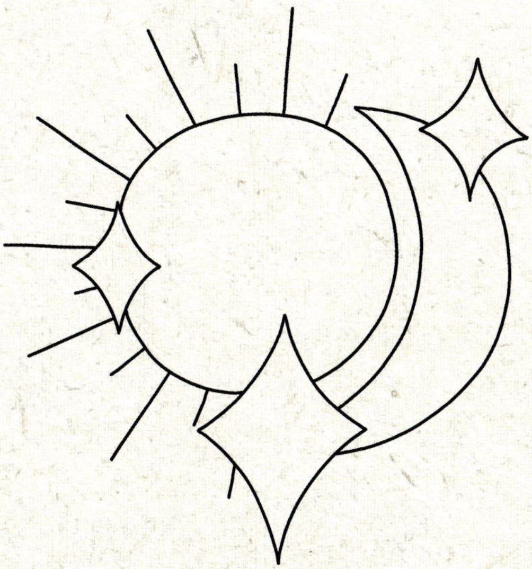

SUN, MOON, AND STARS
Sun & Moon Canvas Tote
page 101

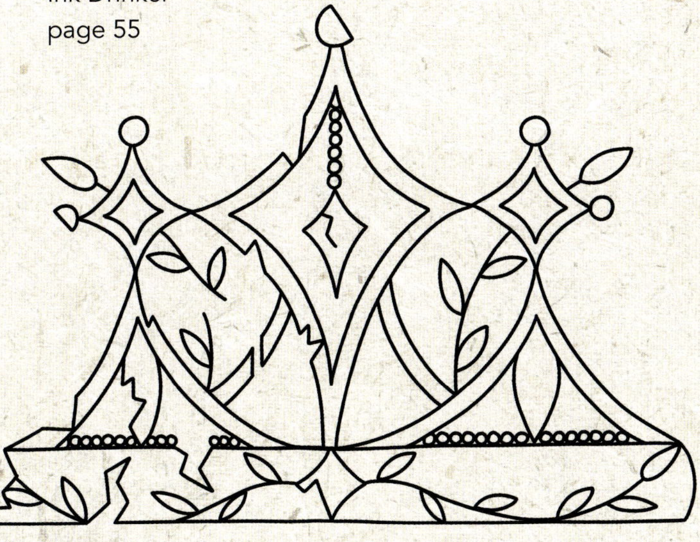

CROWN
Shadow Crown
page 75

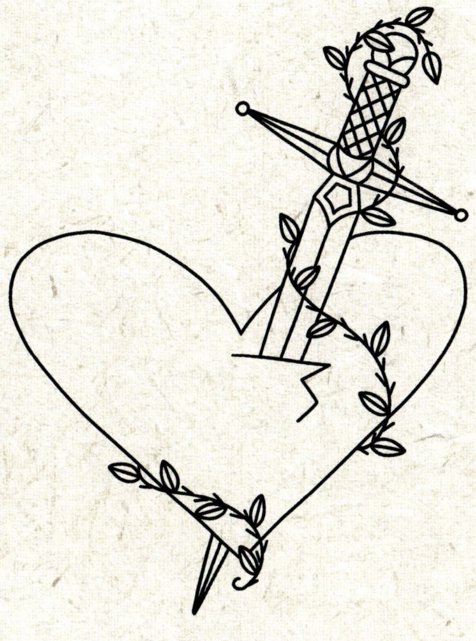

HEART AND SWORD
Enemies to Lovers
page 59

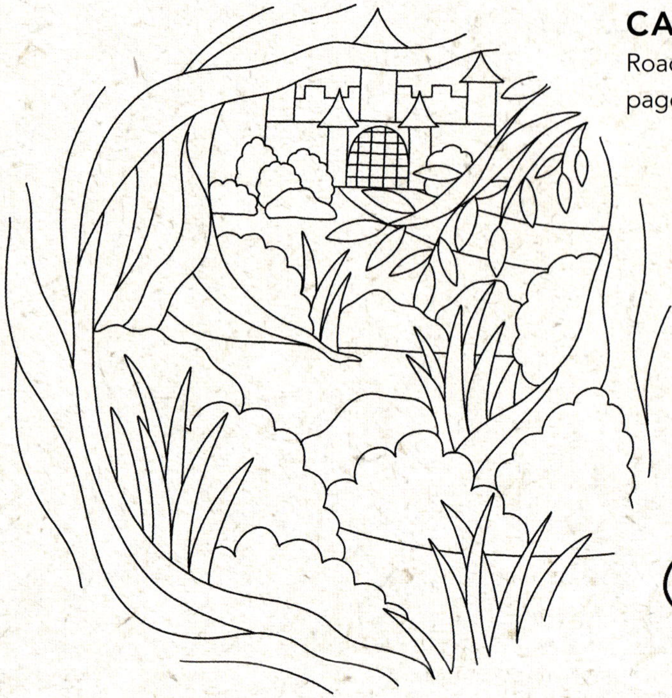

CASTLE
Road to the Castle
page 27

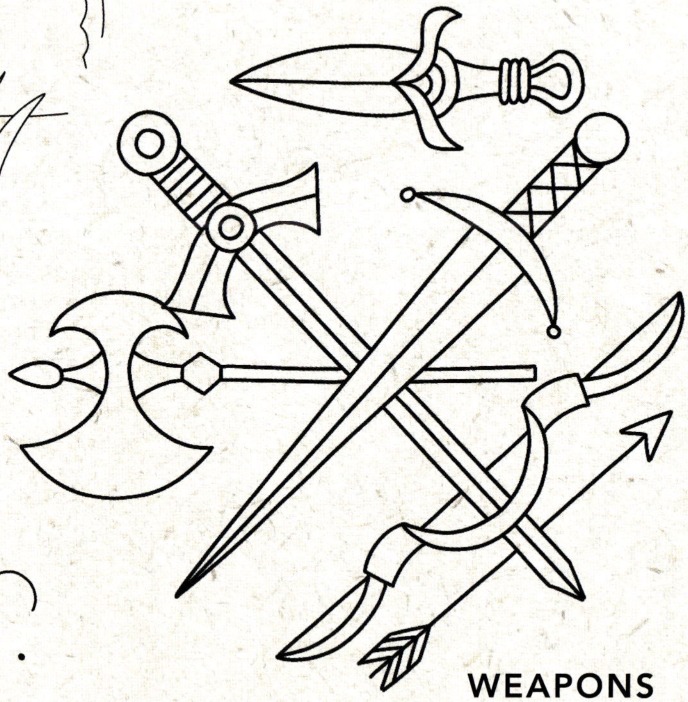

WEAPONS
Self-Rescuing Princess
page 23

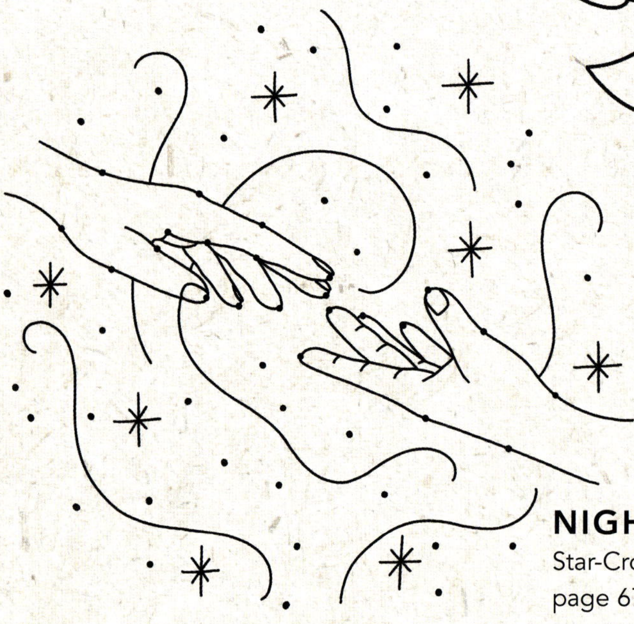

NIGHT SKY
Star-Crossed Romance
page 67

MATCH
Slow Burn Bookmark
page 85

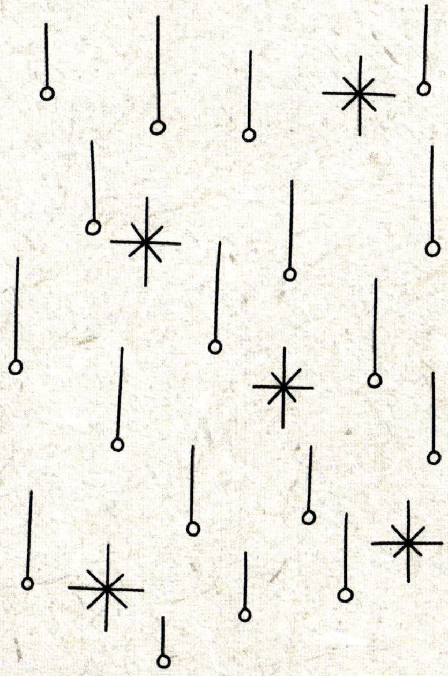

STARFALL
Starfall Needle Book
page 93

HEARTS
Hearts E-Reader Cover
page 97

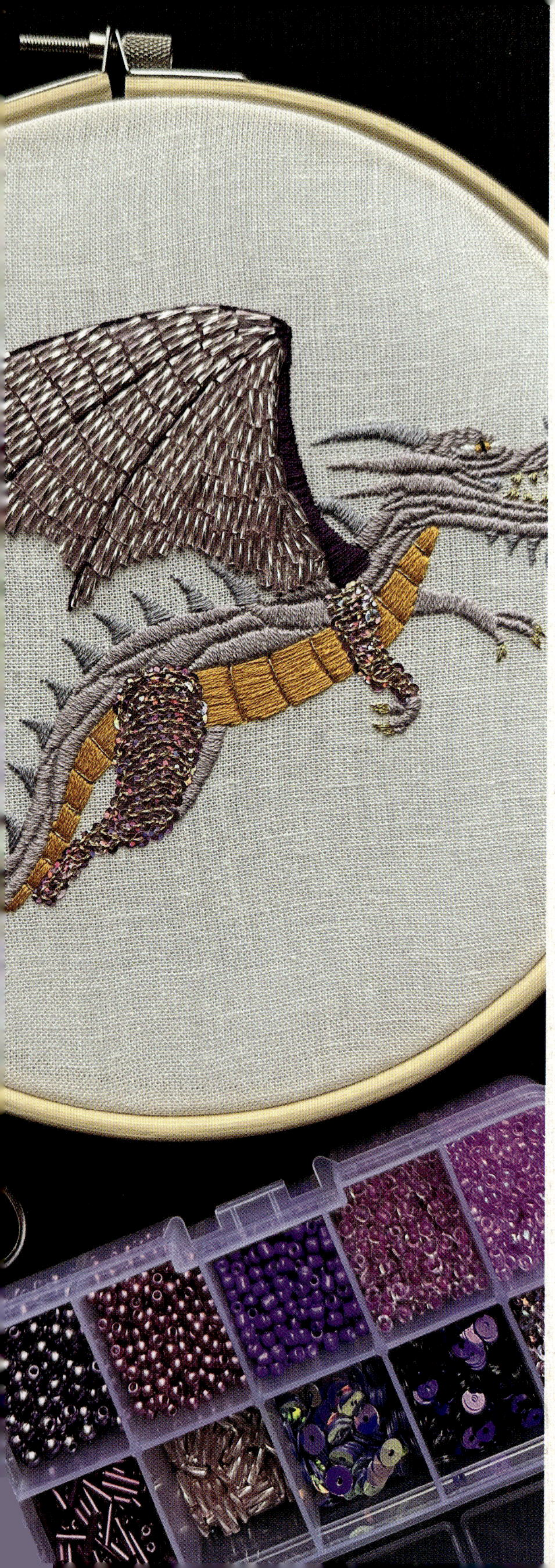

Dedication

For Erin
Thank you for helping me rediscover the joy of reading and for your friendship which means more to me than you know.

Acknowledgments

Thank you, Kerry, for your endless support, encouragement, and belief in my work!

Trudi, the sparkle of your words gives this book the wonderful magic it deserves.

Thank you isn't a strong enough statement to my parents and to Greg for supporting my artistic dreams!

About the Author

Hilary is a self-taught embroidery artist from the Oregon Coast. Though drawing was her main creative outlet since day one, she never looked back once she picked up an embroidery needle in 2020. Hilary's work has since been featured in *Love Embroidery* magazine, *Labores del Hogar*, and Etsy's Pick. You can see more of her work on Instagram and TikTok @hlesliedesign and on Etsy (HLeslieDesign).

Index

Quarto.com

First Published in 2026 by Quarry Books, an imprint of The Quarto Group,
100 Cummings Center, Suite 265-D, Beverly, MA 01915, USA.
T (978) 282-9590 F (978) 283-2742

EEA Representation, WTS Tax d.o.o.,
Žanova ulica 3, 4000 Kranj, Slovenia.
www.wts-tax.si

Quarry Books titles are also available at discount for retail, wholesale, promotional, and bulk purchase. For details, contact the Special Sales Manager by email at specialsales@quarto.com or by mail at The Quarto Group, Attn: Special Sales Manager, 100 Cummings Center, Suite 265-D, Beverly, MA 01915, USA.

10 9 8 7 6 5 4 3 2 1

ISBN: 978-1-57715-817-2

Digital edition published in 2026
eISBN: 978-1-57715-818-9

Library of Congress Cataloging-in-Publication Data
Names: Leslie, Hilary author
Title: A hoop of threads & longing : 20 ink-drinking, slow-burning romantasy embroidery projects-oaths, daggers & stitches for shelf trophies / Hilary Leslie.
Other titles: A hoop of threads and longing
Description: Beverly, MA, USA : Quarry Books, 2026. | Includes index. | Summary: "Embark on a romantasy-inspired embroidery adventure with A Hoop of Threads & Longing-20 story-rich projects blending bookish motifs, celestial symbols, and beginner-friendly techniques"-- Provided by publisher.
Identifiers: LCCN 2025050839 | ISBN 9781577158172 trade paperback | ISBN 9781577158189 ebook
Subjects: LCSH: Embroidery | Embroidery--Patterns
Classification: LCC TT770 .L396 2026 | DDC 746.44/041--dc23/eng/20260116
LC record available at https://lccn.loc.gov/2025050839

Design and page layout: Laura Klynstra
Cover Image: Hilary Leslie

Printed in Guangdong, China TT062026